To Ed Jones,

Good Luck to you &

Catch your their when

friends

HAIL MARY

HAIL MARY

"THE DREW PEARSON STORY"

BY DREW PEARSON

EDITED BY

JIM O. ROGERS

FRANK LUKSA

Zone Press
Denton, Texas

HAIL MARY

"THE DREW PEARSON STORY"

BY DREW PEARSON

Zone Press
an imprint of Rogers Publishing and Consulting, Inc.
109 East Oak – Suite 300
Denton, Texas 76201
info@zonepress.com

Graphic images were created by Ron Meloni and Jim Rogers utilizing photographs from the Drew Pearson Collection

Jim O. Rogers – Editor
Frank Luksa – Editor
Condell Garden – Associate Editor
Lori Walker – Production and Design
Sonja Rogers – Associate Editor
Charlotte Beckham – Copy Edit
Ron Meloni – Cover Design
Alexandria Marx – Promotion and Web Design

Printed in the United States of America
ISBN: 0-9727488-2-2

DEDICATION
★★★★★

The five stars under each chapter heading in this book represent my family members who have passed on. This book is dedicated in loving memory of them.

★My Dad, Samuel
★My Mom, Minnie
★My Brother, Sam
★My Brother, Carey
★My Sister, Debbie

ACKNOWLEDGEMENTS
★★★★★

No man is an island...no man stands alone

My life's journey has not been a lonely one. I am blessed to have been surround by many great people who have touched me in significant ways. Their influence has made an important difference in my life. I thank each of them for their support.

Tori Pearson
Britni Pearson Cannon
Jared Pearson
Kavika Pittman ll
Toren Pittman
Sandra Pearson Hill
Andre Valentino Pearson
Denise Pearson Stewart
Gracie Washington
Obie Washington
Clara Harris
Ethel Scott
George Washington
Frank Washington
Calvin Pearson
Charlie Pearson
Lucy Pearson
Thomas Mickey
Stan Kolo
Louise Garrison
Phil Hill
Gina Pearson
Ernie Scott
Millie Washington Garland
Tootsie Kuzava
Corky Kuzava
Charlie Rains
Rev. H.O. Williams
Ethel Williams
Ms. Carrie Hill
Ella Gray
John Russell
Joe Bellisimo
Hugh Walsh
John Carroll
Dave Briskie
Pauline Ngan
Seaton Higginbothom
"Smokey" John Reeves
Gary Delaune
Rayfield Wright

Chris Cullen
Craig Cullen
Cindy Mickey
Tre' Stewart
Justin Hill
Michele Hill
Ashlee Pearson
Jenna Pearson
Alexandra Pearson
Kyle Wiggins
Josh Wiggins
Carl Hill
Troy Hill
Max Hill
George Haynes
Allan Jones
Arthur Callaway
Eddie Hill
Steve Markman
Al Losiewicz
Skip Hansen
Richie Balasz
Hutch Witkowski
Glenn Berman
Scotty Skarzynski
Stan Graf
Mike Adams
Dr. Lee Bourland
Mary Fisher
Mr. Sam
Ken Shead
Mike Russell
Shannon Vaughan Bennett
Wynne Marko
John Lackenmeyer
Vince McMahon
Harvey Martin
Ms. Helen Martin
Roger Staubach
Jerry "Jambo" Moen
Jethro Pugh

Billy Joe Dupree
Thomas Henderson
Ed "Too Tall" Jones
Tom Landry
Alicia Landry
Tony Dorsett
Robert Newhouse
Doug Donley
Tony Hill
Dick Nolan
Bob Hayes
Leroy Jordan
Bob Lilly
Ron Springs
Aaron Mitchell
Mel Renfro
Walt Garrison
Percy&Gwen Washington
William & Pauline Washington
Sam Pearson lll
Drewan Pearson
Jeffnor Pearson
Seth Pearson
Josh Pearson
Slyvester &Viola Pearson
Dr. Yvonne Bennett
Bishop Eddie Bennett
Dorothy&Richard Mayo
Richard Mickey
Joyce Kosa
Michelle Hill Klausner
Minnie Martin
Dolly Currie
Shirley Poteet
Wayne Bartholomew
Rich Byrd
Inez and Robert Perry
Marsha Haynes Pearson
Marquetta Haynes
Marques Haynes
Jill Lucus

Shuck and Jive
  Board of Directors:
  Forrest, John, Mark,
  Lenny, Jay, Tom, Steve
  Beth, Ivy, The Wrens,
  Desmond and Isabelle,
  Elmo, Bill, Billy, and
  in honor of Doug Staley
Ted Plumb
Doug Cosbie
Roscoe Wiggins
Seaton Higginbothom
Preston Pearson
Jay Saldi
Charlie Waters
Cliff Harris
D.D. Lewis
Calvin Hill
Dale Hansen
Mike Davis
Janie Tilford
Roz Cole
Max Hill Sr.
Florence Jackson
Mary Barnes Knox
Don and Tonya Griffin
Claude Gibson
Lance Cannon
Kavika Pittman
Jim Rogers
Frank Luksa
Zone Press
  Condell, Lori, Sonja,
  Charlotte, Ron &Alex
Willis Johnson
Ralph Anderson
Kara Citrano Leonard
Rick Haba
Bonnie Ricca
Kim Travis
LRS
Otto Stowe

HAIL MARY

FOREWORD
★★★★★

By Roger Staubach

During the off-season in 1973 I worked for the Henry S. Miller real estate company most of the day and went to the practice field late in the afternoon. Few veterans showed up during those hours. Many times the only player working out with me was a rookie free agent wide receiver.

No one thought at first glance that he would survive with the Cowboys. He was skinny, of average height, weighed no more than 180 pounds and lacked great speed. These non-threatening looks eventually served as his camouflage for 11 NFL seasons. He didn't look the part of a future All-Pro and three-time Pro Bowl honoree. As defensive backs learned too late, he didn't look fast or elusive.

Therein lay the secret of Drew Pearson's remarkable career. He thrived on deception. His façade telegraphed innocence to opponents.

But Drew didn't fool me long. I caught on to him before anyone else did through all our pre-training camp time together.

We often worked out by ourselves. I threw and he caught. It didn't take long to realize he caught everything I threw.

I knew Drew was serious about football. He moved to Dallas to prepare himself. He worked harder than other rookies.

Drew's athletic skills became apparent. He had excellent body control. His hands were soft and supple. He caught passes high, low and to either side. The way he moved on the field was so instinctive that it made me think, *This kid from Tulsa has something special.*

And he did. Drew was football smart. He ran precise routes. He knew how to adjust in the midst of confusion. He was tough, wiry and durable. He had no fear of going over the middle. He caught in a crowd or if he couldn't, he defended against an interception. He could find the right seam in a defense.

Yet in a unique way, Drew was handicapped for at least half of his career. After Tony Dorsett joined us in 1977 we had so many offensive weapons Drew suffered personally because we didn't have to throw 40 passes a game to win. Drew's statistics are Ring of Honor and Pro Football Hall of Fame worthy, but they could have been gaudy.

Until Dorsett arrived, we won many games with big plays and Drew made most of them. A partial list of his game-deciding catches included an 83-yard touchdown pass from me to clinch the '73 divisional playoff against the Los Angeles Rams. The next year it was a 50-yarder from Clint Longley to nip Washington in the last minute, 24-23. In '75 he and I connected on the Hail Mary against Minnesota. In '78 he caught two fourth quarter touchdowns from Danny White to beat Atlanta 27-20 in a playoff.

The Hail Mary remains the most famous play in Cowboys history and might as well have been drawn in the dirt. We made it up in the huddle from the 50-yard line. I told Drew to fake our favorite pattern, the 16 Route, where he ran 16 yards and slanted over the middle. Only this time, he was to break the route and cut deep. I said I'd pump fake the opposite way to draw free safety Paul Krause away from the area and let fly. I basically told everyone else to block.

Typical Drew caught my under thrown pass in a tangle with Nate Wright around the 5-yard line with 24 seconds left to play. I was hit as I threw so I didn't see the touchdown that beat the Vikings in a divisional playoff, 17-14. But I knew something good had happened for us. There were no cheers from the Minnesota crowd.

That game changed Dallas Cowboys history. We went to three Super Bowls within a span of four years from '75 to '78. A free agent receiver who made that play helped us to become America's Team. And he got me into the Hall of Fame.

HAIL MARY

PROLOGUE

★★★★★

December 28th, 1975

Metropolitan Stadium

Bloomington, Minnesota

It was the first round of the playoffs and the Minnesota Vikings were heavy favorites over the wild card Dallas Cowboys. The Doomsday Defense and The Purple People Eaters had fought to a 10-7 Dallas lead for most of four quarters. With 1:51 left in the game, Fran Tarkenton and the Minnesota offense scored to go ahead 14 -10. With the great Viking defense on the field and the Cowboys starting from their own 15, the home crowd was savoring thoughts of a third straight trip to the NFC Championship game.

Roger Staubach moved us to midfield in nine plays. But we were out of time-outs and there were fewer than 30 seconds on the game clock. One sack or even a completion in the middle of the field, and time would be exhausted.

We lined up in shotgun formation. Roger took the snap, pump-faked left, then turned to his right and fired the ball deep down field. I was out there, being shadowed by Nate Wright. We both turned to the outside to follow the flight of the ball and I cut under him. He slipped on the frozen turf but was still in position to stop the pass. As the ball came down, there was contact but I trapped the ball against my hip at the 5-yard line and somehow backed into the end zone.

In a post-game interview, someone described the play to Roger, who had been hit immediately after throwing the ball and didn't see its ending. "You mean Drew caught the pass and ran in for the touchdown?" Roger asked. "I just threw the ball as far as I could and said a **'Hail Mary'**."

This play defined me as a football player and "Hail Mary" became a part of sports vernacular. It also became part of my philosophy of life. I believe that everyone gets a few Hail Marys in life and that if we prepare ourselves and work hard enough, we might catch a few of them.

My life has been about overcoming difficult odds but at the same time it has been blessed. I was a skinny kid who believed he could play in the National Football League despite the fact that I weighed only 160 pounds, wasn't very fast, and had played only two years as a wide receiver at the University of Tulsa.

Looking back on it I've had several Hail Marys come my way and I like to think that because of my confidence and the work ethic instilled in me by my parents and teachers, I've caught most of them. I hope my story inspires you to prepare yourself to catch the Hail Marys that come your way........*Drew Pearson 88*

SOUTH RIVER

HAIL MARY
CHAPTER ONE
★★★★★

My mother and father both came from big families. There were five kids in Dad's and seven in Mom's. I guess that led to us having a big family. There were seven of us kids. I was born in Newark, New Jersey, and we lived in the Newark area when I was very young.

When I was three we moved to a three-story house in South River, New Jersey, on Prospect Street. Prospect Street was known for two things. First, it was known for the pond where everyone skated. The big pond was in the park, right across the street from where we lived. It was fantastic. People would come from all over to skate in the winter and swim in the summer. The other thing it was known for was the curve. When you came off the hill on Prospect Street, there was a sharp curve. Our house was to the left of the curve. Every night, going to bed was an adventure because we would always hear screeching car tires and sometimes there were accidents. There was a pole right in front of our house and I don't know how many times people ran into that pole because they couldn't navigate the curve.

We didn't live in the three-story house by ourselves. Aunt Dolly and Uncle William Mickey and their kids Helen, Richard, Thomas and Dorothy lived on the first floor. A single lady, Margie Brown, lived by herself on the third floor. We lived in the middle on the second floor. There were two bedrooms in our section of the house; the girls had a bedroom and the boys had a bedroom. My parents turned the dining room, which was in the middle between the living room and the kitchen, into the master bedroom. To get to our rooms or to go to the kitchen we were constantly walking through our parent's bedroom.

My family included an older brother, Sam, and older sister, Sandra. I was the third one in line. Next were younger brother Andre, sister Denise, brother Carey and baby sister Debbie. A baby sister Sharon, born between Andre and me, died at birth.

My father emphasized sports with the boys and it was natural for us to be involved with football, basketball, and baseball. Sam set the precedent. He played all of the sports, and because he was playing, I was motivated and wanted to play. My first year of playing organized football was when I was seven years old in the Edison, Pop Warner league. I was with the pee wee team. We weren't even big enough to wear football pants.

Growing up, nothing interested me except sports. Even at the age of seven all I wanted to do was play ball.

Baseball was my favorite sport, but I also played football and basketball. When I think back on my childhood, being involved in sports is most of what I remember. I remember some things with the family, hanging out together. My dad used to barbecue all of the time and that was a big thing. All of our relatives would get together and come down from Newark, Jersey City, Keyport and Matawan. Family was big with us, not just the immediate family but also all the extended family including Mom's and Dad's brothers and sisters and their kids.

My dad, Samuel Pearson, Sr., was a good man and a hard-working man but he was a tough man. He was a harsh disciplinarian. I'm sure he had a lot of pressure on him raising seven kids and sometimes he took that pressure out on us through his discipline. Of course, back then we didn't like it or appreciate it. Now as we look back, we think we are what we are because of how we were raised and disciplined.

Dad grew up in a big family with a lot of brothers. He was the youngest and was always a hard worker. He worked as a weigher for an agricultural company. As the trains and trucks would come to the ports along the New Jersey coastline, he would help unload them. He worked his way up to foreman.

He was a sophisticated man and liked to wear a suit and tie. His work, of course, wasn't conducive to that kind of attire. But away from work, at church, hanging out or dealing with his political interests, he always wore a suit and tie. He was interested in the political atmosphere. At one time he held a position at the Middlesex County Equal Opportunity Corporation. He was involved in many political organizations on a local basis and that seemed to consume more of Dad than his job. I never really saw him that much in overalls or coveralls, which were his normal work clothes. When we went to church all the boys would wear suits and ties. His rule was, "Don't ever take that jacket off until you take your tie off." I think a lot of the things I do today, the way I dress and care about my appearance, are because of the way my father dressed and cared about his. He was always concerned about how he presented himself when he stepped out of the house.

Dad was an extremely physical man. He felt that the best way to discipline his kids was through physical punishment. All of us feared him. We feared him and did not want to upset him. We did not want to let him down, whether it was in our chores around the house, our grades in school, or on the playing field. I found out later that I had that same kind of fear, in a different way, for Coach Tom Landry. I wasn't afraid that Coach Landry would hit me but I desperately needed his approval. I used the same kind of motivation in winning the approval of Coach Landry that I used winning the approval of my dad. I never wanted either one of them to be disappointed in me. When I was trying to make the Cowboys, my primary objective was to please Coach Landry.

Mom's approval was also important. She was a "no nonsense" person but she would talk to us and discipline us through words. The fear was greater with Dad but both of them provided motivation for us to want to do right and be successful.

Dad was a hard man. I think it made all of us hard, including my sisters. There was no separation of discipline between the boys and the girls. We all were in the same pot. We all got the same punishment, and it was mostly physical. Today, parents probably couldn't get away with my dad's kind of punishment and they probably shouldn't.

Dad named his first son, Sam, after himself, and I have no idea who my sister Sandra was named for. When it came to me, his second son, I guess he had to figure out something different. Dad admired the political journalist, Drew Pearson, who operated out of Washington, D.C. and wrote a syndicated column. The column, called the *Washington Merry-Go-Round*, appeared daily in his favorite paper, the *Newark Star Ledger*. I was named after Drew Pearson. As a kid, I didn't know who Drew Pearson was. I would see the paper and his name but I didn't read the articles and didn't know who he was because he wasn't on the sports page. I got to appreciate him later because in school, every time the roll call would come around to my name, I'd raise my hand and the teacher would say, "Are you named after the columnist?" I figured this guy must be pretty popular and lot of people must know who he is. That kind of thing embarrassed me, however, and so did the name. No one else around was named Drew. It was an easy name to tease. They called me Draws and other crazy names at school and I didn't have a middle name. Drew Pearson the columnist was just Drew Pearson. He didn't have a middle name and I didn't either. I was the only one in the family with no middle name. I didn't like my name. I wanted to have a good sports name like Reggie, Brian or Lance.

I didn't learn to accept Drew until I got to the NFL and decided it was cool because no one else was named Drew. At first I didn't like it because no one was named Drew, then I *liked* it because no one was named Drew.

Because my Dad named me Drew Pearson, he expected certain things from me. He expected me to get all A's and do everything right. He expected me to be the perfect child. Even though Sam was named after him, my father seemed to put more pressure on me because my name was Drew Pearson. He had a thing for boy's names. My younger brother's name is Andre Valentino. *Drew Pearson and Andre Valentino*...Back in those days, a black youngster named Drew or Andre was unique. I guess after Andre, my mom took over naming the rest of the kids; at least their names were more normal. That's when Denise, Carey and Debbie came into the picture.

My mom was great -- Mary Minnie Lee Washington Pearson Schenck. She was an unbelievable person. She was very caring, supportive and hard working. Mom worked by cleaning other people's homes. She would walk to work and clean upper class houses in South River. While she and dad were at work, we were home alone. That's how we learned to do things. If we wanted something to eat, we had to cook it. If we wanted a shirt washed and ironed, we had to wash and iron it. To this day, I'm a good ironer, washer, cook and grocery shopper. I learned at an early age to be self-sufficient.

My mom played basketball and softball. When I was young, I didn't realize that she was an athlete, she was just Mom. Dad pushed us to play sports and mom supported us. When I started playing Little League baseball, we had an annual event. Our team played a game in the morning and in the afternoon the parents played each other. My mom got out there and I thought, *She's going to get hurt or embarrass me*. The first time she was at bat, she smashed the ball against the left field fence and the next time up she hit it over the fence. As she ran around the bases I couldn't believe it was my mother.

She was the star of the game and after the game I said, "Mom. I didn't know you could play like that."

She said, "Yeah, I used to play a little ball." Of course, she was low-key about it. I'd given dad all the credit for my athletic ability, but when I saw mom play I knew that I got it from her too. She played in all-star games, parents against kids, and she was the star.

After living in South River for five or six years, we moved to Edison. This was a big move for us because we had a house to ourselves with a large yard and an upstairs. It was a big moment for the Pearson family when we moved into the house. It was a prideful moment for my dad to be able to qualify and get the house.

Life was great in Edison for a while, but over a period of time my dad started doing crazy stuff. I guess the pressure got to him. He drank a lot, did some irresponsible things and was violent around the house. It got to a point that when Friday rolled around, us kids hoped and prayed that he wouldn't come home that night. A lot of nights he wouldn't come home. If he did, however, he'd be drunk and we never knew what he would do. We always hoped he would come home the next day sober and in a better state of mind.

Even though we lived in Edison, we still went to church in South River at the Union Baptist Church. Because he was constantly getting lost in some escapade, sometimes Dad wouldn't come home and we wouldn't have a ride to church. Our pastor, H.O. Williams, lived in Piscataway, New Jersey, which is on the other side of Edison. Reverend and Mrs. Williams would pick us up and take us to church. That was good, but it had one small catch. Reverend Williams had to stay there all day. From eight in the morning until four o'clock in the afternoon we were at church because we had to wait until he got through to get a ride home. Reverend Williams was a great man and pastored that church for more than fifty years.

CHAPTER TWO
★★★★★

My mom and dad divorced just before I entered my freshman year of high school. That's when we moved from Edison back to South River. Mom took all seven kids and left, and we had no idea where we were going. Through the Union Baptist Church, she was able to get a house in South River. The church had moved from its original location on the causeway, and she rented a house next to the new church.

As kids, we didn't know what was going on. We could see the tension between our parents, and we were concerned. We were worried, mostly for our mother. Dad was gone all of the time and mom was always there when she wasn't working. My mom made a decision that she was going to leave and that she wasn't leaving by herself. She was going to take all of her kids. We were shocked when she came to us and said that we were leaving.

At first, when the separation happened, we were mad at mom. We thought it was her fault. We thought she was the one breaking up the family. But in reality she was making the family better and getting out of a bad situation.

Still, we loved our dad. No matter how he dealt with us, we loved him immensely and cared for him. When Mom first left, we didn't all move to South River right away. She had to build up some cash flow, work out the arrangements on the house, and wait until the church purchased the new church building and house. In the meantime, the family was split. Debbie, Carey and Mom moved in with Aunt Ethel, my mom's sister, in New Brunswick, New Jersey. The rest of us moved down the street with a friend, Mary Fisher and her family. We stayed there for about a month. Believe me, that was devastating. We kept thinking, *Why is mom doing this?* We couldn't understand what was going on. When she finally worked the deal to get the house in South River, it brought us all together just before the start of the school year.

My freshman year was going to be a big year for me because when had I started my seventh grade year in Edison, I was diagnosed with Osgood Schlatters Disease. Osgood Schlatters is a bone disease that occurs mostly in young kids. My nephew Trey has it now. It is a disease that causes swelling, pain and tenderness just below the knee over the shin bone. I was playing a lot of baseball at that time and I was a catcher. I would come home and be in severe pain after each game. Back then you didn't know anything about ice and didn't have Advil, so you dealt with the pain by accepting it. Dad knew about it, but he never took me to the doctor. Mom couldn't take me because she couldn't afford to pay a doctor to find out what was wrong. Finally, my uncle, Ernie Scott, Aunt Ethel's husband, took me to the doctor and he diagnosed me with Osgood Schlatter Disease. He said that the only way to cure it or deal with it and prevent the pain was to rest. He told me not to play any more ball. It was hard to take.

I half-heartedly accepted and went through it. I couldn't be on the school teams but it was difficult not to be active. I had to wear braces on my knees all of the time. While the other kids were playing, I just sat there and watched. I did accept it for a while, but I couldn't accept it forever. I started sneaking out and playing ball with my buddies at the schoolyard. The summer after my eighth-grade year, without my parents knowing it, I played in a summer recreational tournament and we won the tournament. I was named the most valuable player, and I got two trophies that I couldn't take home because my dad would see them and punish me. So I had to give them to my buddy, Nicky Genova. I told Nicky, "You save these for me. One day I'll come back and get 'em," but I never did.

Starting my freshman year the doctors finally said I could play ball again. Mom got the family together and we moved to South River, in a big white house right next to the church. It was a nice house. It had a front porch and we each had our own room. I knew a little bit about South River because of my early days growing up there.

Mom was still working hard at this point but was no longer cleaning houses. She got a job at E.R. Squibb & Son, which was a pharmaceutical company in New Brunswick. It was a big move for her. Now she had a regular paycheck and benefits. She ended up working for Squibb almost 30 years.

Mom passed away in 2001 of a heart attack at the age of 78. She had been going strong. She was on her way to church for choir practice to pick out new choir robes when she died. She was the driver going to pick up a group of her girlfriends. She pulled in the driveway of her first girlfriend, Carrie Hill. Carrie was my sister's mother-in-law. Mom usually didn't get out of the car. She would just beep and her girlfriends were always ready because she didn't like to wait. This time, however, she pulled in the driveway, got out of the car and was taking her first step. She fell back and that was it. She had a heart attack and died right there.

My mom was an icon in South River. Everyone knew her. For her funeral, the town was deserted. South River came to a standstill. The night before the funeral the family greeted friends at the church starting at five o'clock. We stayed there until nine. The whole time people were coming into the Union Baptist Church we had known as kids. The house we grew up in was still right there, All these people from the town, white, black, young kids, old kids, adults, came through the whole night. The town was in shock that she had passed away.

While I was growing up there, South River had a population of about 15,000. In that area, if you go a mile you're in the next town. All of the towns are connected. People came not only from South River and East Brunswick, they came from Perth, Amboy, New Brunswick, and every town around just to pay their respects to my mom.

The next day at the funeral, the church was packed and people were standing outside. My mom did everything in that community. She was involved with volunteer work, voter registration, political work, church work, sports, and booster clubs. When she passed away it was something that not only the town but the whole area felt. The funeral procession, I remember, was so long that it was difficult keeping the cars together on the way to the cemetery.

CHAPTER THREE
★★★★★

When we moved to South River we realized why mom moved and why it was necessary for us to be separated for a short time. We came to love, respect and appreciate our mother more than ever. She got out of a situation that wasn't comfortable for her and wasn't best for her kids. She moved the seven kids out of there. We were fragmented for a while but she got us back together. At the same time, we were staying in touch with our dad. Whenever we had an athletic event or special occasion, he was there.

At the time, my brother Sam was a senior football player at Edison high school. I think they won one football game. They were a pretty bad team, but he was the star running back. Even though we were in South River, he stayed with a friend in Edison so he could complete his senior year there. Sam was a little crazy. He bought old cars for twenty bucks and drove them as far as they would take him. Wherever they broke down, he took the license plates off and left them. He went back and forth between Edison and South River in old cars. I can't tell you how many cars I saw him drive to the house. Old pieces of junk…. but that was his transportation.

Sam ended up getting a scholarship because he was a great athlete. He was probably the best athlete of all four boys in the family. He could run fast and jump high. He played on the Edison High basketball, football and track teams and went to Western Kentucky on a track and football scholarship.

He was three years older than me. At Western Kentucky he played football and eventually was the captain. The Cincinnati Bengals drafted him in the 17th round as a defensive back.

Just before he went to training camp, he was working at a day care center and tried to open a window that was stuck. He pounded it to loosen the frame. When he did, his hand went through the glass and cut all the nerves and tendons in his wrist. This was about a week before he reported to camp. He was lucky that surgeons were able to mend it together. He went to training camp with virtually one hand and still almost made the team. He didn't make the final cut with the Bengals.

Sam was a phenomenal track athlete in college and I think he could have been a decathlon athlete. He ran the hundred, high hurdles, intermediate hurdles, did the high jump, the long jump, and ran the relays in every track meet. The incredible thing was that he would place in all of them.

After the incident with his hand, he tried some minor league football and then ended up coaching. He was a very good coach. If he had stayed in there, there is no question in my mind that he could have made it to the professional level, or to the college level as a head coach. I always looked up to Sam and thought he was the greatest. When he would come home from Edison to South River, we would all be excited to see him. He passed away in 2000 of a heart attack. He was 52 when he died.

Harvey Martin, my best friend and former Cowboys teammate, passed away in December of 2001 and almost two weeks to the day after my mom died, my aunt Ethel passed away. Then six months later my baby sister died from breast cancer.

I don't want to fluff anything. I don't want anyone to think it's been a bed of roses. Drew Pearson's life is about over-achieving and overcoming adversities. I never used my parents' divorce, the way our dad treated us, the physical abuse, or the Osgood Schlatters as an excuse for not being able to succeed or to do what I wanted to do. A lot of kids nowadays say, "I can't do this because my mom's a drug addict." "I can't do this because I don't know who my dad is." Give me a break. I understand a tough situation, but those are their mistakes, not yours. It doesn't mean you have to make the same mistakes. Instead, learn from their mistakes and try to avoid falling into the same situation. Everyone has to deal with certain situations in life and it's up to the individual to overcome them or roll with them.

CHAPTER FOUR
★★★★★

When I entered South River High School, the doctors released me to play ball again. I couldn't wait to start. It was my freshman year and I was gung ho. Since I'd just returned to South River and hadn't played in a while; nobody knew who I was. When the coach asked for the positions I wanted to play, I told him, "I want to play quarterback and middle linebacker."

He asked, "Why?"

I said, "I haven't been playing for a couple of years and I want to be in the middle of the action."

I had never thought about playing quarterback because I always wanted to be a wide receiver. But I wanted to be in the focal point of the action. I told coach I wanted to be a quarterback and a middle linebacker and that's where I played as a high school freshman.

I was active as a middle linebacker. I weighed 140 - 145 pounds, but I was tall, maybe 5'10, 5'11…. tall and skinny. As middle linebacker, I could read those guards. Back then the guards would pull. If a guard pulled and the tackle blocked down, I knew they were pulling for the sweep. I was so quick and skinny that when that guard would pull, I would shoot the gap and be in the backfield before the other team could react. I never had enough "oomph" to really hit anybody, so I'd just grab their ankles and hold on until my teammates came and finished them off. I was the skinniest, most non-physical middle linebacker in the history of football. At quarterback I did fairly well. The team had a great year. I don't remember what the record was, but we won a lot more games than we lost.

I also played basketball my freshman year. We had a great coach, John Fuerher. I say he was great because he stressed fundamentals. I mean, that's all we did … dribbling, passing, catching, setting picks and pick and roll fundamentals. Before then I had played some basketball but it was mostly, "throw the ball out there and shoot." It was good having a coach like Coach Fuerher. He was strict and hard and that was what I was used to. I fell right in with him and we had a good basketball season.

I remember one time that he benched me for dunking before a game. Dunking in warm ups was popular then because it was against the rules to do it in the game. We constantly tried to dunk. We put stick-um on our hands so we could palm the ball. But try as we might, we couldn't dunk it. One of my teammates was Scotty Skarzynski. Scotty was a big freshman. He was at least 6'2 and he couldn't even dunk.

In spite of our futile efforts, Scotty and I came up with a plan to dunk before a home game with Perth Amboy. I ran and got a chair and placed it in front of the basket. Scotty leaped off the chair and dunked the ball. He then held the chair for me as I dunked. Coach was furious and ended up benching both of us before the game. My dad was also mad. He wanted to kick my butt.

I had a good freshman year playing baseball. I loved baseball and my dream was to play in the big leagues. I had started out as a catcher in little league. I liked putting on the mask and picturing myself as Elston Howard. I loved the idea of strapping on the shin guards and putting that chest protector on. It felt like I was more a part of the game than anybody else because I had the equipment on. The first glove my dad bought me was a catcher's mitt. When you're playing with the kids out in the street, what good is a catcher's mitt? You don't even have a catcher in street ball so I played in the field with my catcher's mitt.

Once I got into high school and freshman ball, I grew out of the catcher's position because the effect Osgood Schlatters had on my knees. I became a shortstop and center fielder.

In my last year of Little League, back in Edison before we moved, our team was undefeated. The coach used to let me bat first so I'd get more at bats. I batted over .900 in my last year in Little League.

CHAPTER FIVE

★★★★★

Going into my sophomore year, I had a chance to start on the varsity in all three sports: football, basketball, and baseball. In football, Joe Theismann was the quarterback (Joey was Thees-mann back then. I think they changed the pronunciation to Thighs-mann when he went to Notre Dame so it would rhyme with Heisman). I made the team as a sophomore. I backed up at wide receiver, started at safety and backed up Joey at quarterback. We finished the season undefeated at 9-0. We were un-scored on in six games.

During my first game as a sophomore, the starting wide receiver got hurt, so I went in. On the first play Joey called a pass play in a huddle. I don't remember the terminology we used, but I was to run a post pattern. Joey took the snap and I ran the post pattern as he scrambled around. He went to his right. Then he spun to the left, acting like he was going to run with the ball. Then he threw that ball 60 yards in the air, a perfect spiral, and I was standing in the end zone waiting for it to come down. When it finally came down, I caught it. It was a 60-yard touchdown. The first pass I caught as a high school football player was a 60-yard touchdown from Joe Theismann.

I would play the varsity games, never coming off the field. Then I would play the J. V. game on Monday at quarterback so I could get groomed to replace Joey after he graduated. I played two games a week and wished that I could play another. I thought, *This is kind of fun. It sure beats practice.*

I had a ritual before every game to walk downtown, which was a block from where we lived, (downtown only lasted about a block anyway.) My mom would give me a couple of bucks and I would go to the Ben Franklin five and dime store. I wore black Adidas shoes, and I bought new white shoelaces and white socks.   As I walked through town, people honked their horns and yelled, "Good luck today!" "Let's get'em today!" Let's beat East Brunswick!" Football was big in South River, New Jersey.

We had a great sophomore year and ended up ranked third in the state. We didn't have playoffs back then, just state rankings. Our coach was Ron Wojicki. Coach Wojicki was tough! He was a disciplinarian. He would push us hard by making us run. Our school was on top of a hill and it was 40 yards nearly straight up. We would run up, come back down, and run up again. That was part of our discipline. It was hard being a South River football player, but if you were a boy growing up there, that's what you dreamed of doing. Baseball and basketball were important, but because of the glory of playing football for the South River Rams, they were not as important as football. To be on that football team with seniors like Joe Theismann, Andy Evano, Chink Malinowski and Carl Hill was a great experience.

We played against Linden, New Jersey, in my sophomore year and they had a great running back. He broke away and I chased him. I played free safety and played real deep. The only tackles I made were if someone was loose in the secondary and we had such a great defensive front that seldom happened. I ended up grabbing the guy by his shoulder pads at the 2-yard line and yanked him backwards to keep him from going into the end zone. We held them four plays and protected our scoreless game streak. After the game, the coach jumped all over me. "You're supposed to get in front of the guys and hit 'em. You're not supposed to grab 'em from behind." But that's how I tackled, even when I was part of the Cowboys' special teams. I wasn't big enough to be sticking my head in there. I would go around the blocking wedge and get the ball carrier from behind. Coach Landry didn't like it either. "You're supposed to be bustin' through the wedge," he would say.

After Joey graduated, I became the quarterback and still played free safety on defense. I had a good season. We lost two games. We were 6-2-1 that year and those are the only two games I lost in my high school career. One game I lost because I threw six interceptions against Highland Park. They ate me up and I couldn't wait to get them the next year. East Brunswick beat us as well. Scotty Skarzynski was my favorite receiver. He was about 6'4" by this time. He ended up going to Penn State as a wide receiver and played in the Cotton Bowl against Texas in 1972.

My senior year, we were stacked with talent. The first game of the season we played the Highland Park team that had beat us the previous year when I threw the six interceptions. The first play of the game I sprinted out right and took it all the way to the end zone. I don't remember the final score but we ended up beating them pretty bad and I got my revenge.

Our senior year we were 8-0-1. We tied the last game of the season with our arch rival New Brunswick. It was the big game on Thanksgiving Day at Rutgers University Stadium. We dominated the game, and beat them everywhere but on the scoreboard. I had a punt return called back because the official said I stepped out of bounds. I took the ball, backtracked and came down the sideline and no one was left but the kicker. I was going to run over him or cut inside him. But he threw himself at me, trying to cut me from underneath and I hurdled the guy, like Renaldo Nehemiah Wilson and ran into the end zone. We all went crazy because we thought we won the game. The ref called it back because he said I stepped out and we ended up tied. To New Brunswick it was a victory but to us it was devastating, and I was crying like a baby. We could have finished ranked number one in the state. We ended up number five because of that damn tie. After the game, all of my family consoled me and I thought, *I'll never let this game hurt me like this again.*

You know what? I never cried after another football game until 1981 when Dwight Clark caught that damn ball in San Francisco. I bawled like a baby after that game but after that I thought, *I'll never let football hurt me again.*

I made all-state quarterback and was highly recruited, but not by the same schools as Scotty. Penn State didn't call me. Notre Dame didn't call me. Schools like North Carolina, North Carolina State, Boston College, Rutgers, Nebraska, Michigan State, and Tulsa made contact.

I enjoyed high school football. It was a tremendous experience. Our coach when I was a junior and senior was Joe Bellissimo. He was a great coach. The discipline he set formulated a lot of the guidelines I still follow today.

CHAPTER SIX
★★★★★

We were mediocre in basketball when I was in high school but I loved to play. My sophomore year Joey and I were the backcourt. Joey was the star on the basketball team. He'd be the first to tell you. He's kind of like that. Joe Theismann growing up was, I'm not going to say arrogant…., but a very confident kid. He was confident in his abilities and he had that outgoing type personality. He was always talking and it was usually about himself. We nicknamed him the "black hole" because every time we passed him the ball, we'd never get it back.

Our junior year, they switched basketball coaches and brought in a guy named Jim Ladley from Rahway, New Jersey, which is a tough part of Jersey, and he was a tough guy. He had played pretty serious basketball himself. He was about 6'9", a decent coach but not much of a disciplinarian. Now that Joey was gone, Scotty and I were the stars. We pretty much ran the team. As a matter of fact, Jim Ladley approached Scotty and me in our senior year. Because his job was on the line with the Board of Education, he offered us $10 apiece for every victory. Back then you didn't hear much about scandals. Scotty and I were thinking, *We've got no money, Damn, let's do it*. The last thing coach said before we agreed to do it was, "Don't tell anybody." So we didn't tell. He ended up paying us $100 apiece, $10 a game. Nobody ever knew about it but coach, Scotty, and me. As a matter of fact, this is the first time it has been revealed and Scotty is probably saying, "What the hell you tellin' that for?"

CHAPTER SEVEN

★★★★★

I spent a lot of time by myself in the schoolyard with my baseball and a glove. I would get a piece of chalk, draw a strike out box on the wall, and pitch. I'd pretend I was striking out the New York Yankees line up — Mickey Mantle, Roger Maris, Elston Howard, and Hector Lopez. I was a shy and introverted kid and I think the fact that I spent so much time throwing baseballs and shooting hoops made me a good athlete with supple hands. I tell kids now, "It's not so much what you do when the coach tells you to practice that makes a difference. It's what you do on your own when no one's around and no one's watching."

Thomas Mickey, my cousin who was quite a bit older than me, played on a men's summer league team. He would take me with him to the games. One day they were short a player, so they asked me to play. They stuck me in right field and I got a couple of hits and made some good catches. The next thing I knew, I was on the team at 14 years old.

They played their games mostly on Sunday afternoon and

traveled in North Jersey, South Jersey, and sometimes up in Connecticut. My mom didn't like that because I was missing church on Sunday. I would come home knowing I was going to be in trouble for missing church. But, I would go play, come home and take my whipping, and then do it again the next week. I guess Mom got tired of whipping me because one day she said, "This baseball must really mean something to you." She agreed to let me play baseball if I would go to church on Wednesday evenings. I went to church every Wednesday evening, and that freed me up on Sunday to go play ball with my cousin.

Going into my senior year, I went from shortstop to center field. I had a good senior year, batting in the 300's. I got a chance to sign with the Atlanta Braves out of high school. They picked me in the free agency draft. That, to me, was like a dream come true. All I wanted was an opportunity to play major league baseball, but my dad wouldn't let me sign. He said, "If it's there now, it will be there down the road."

I was obviously disappointed about not being allowed to sign with the Braves but at the same time several colleges were recruiting me to play football. Nebraska was hot for me to replace Jerry Tagge at quarterback. Monte Kiffin, now the great defensive coordinator for the Tampa Bay Bucs, was the guy in charge of recruiting New Jersey at the time. Michigan State, North Carolina State, Boston College, Rutgers, and Tulsa University were also recruiting me.

I was built like a baseball player. I was only about 145 pounds my senior year in high school. I certainly didn't look like a football player. I never lifted any weights in high school. Weight programs weren't that big of a deal back then. We had one universal gym, and some of the guys would get on it and pump some iron, but not me. I never lifted any weights. I was built to be a baseball player and wanted to stay that way.

I played football because there was tremendous pressure from my dad and the community to play. I really wanted to sign with the Atlanta Braves but when my dad said, "No"!, I started thinking about moving on to college. I wanted to find a school that would allow me to play baseball as well as football. Nebraska, North Carolina State, Boston College, Rutgers, and other schools, wouldn't consider letting me play baseball but The University of Tulsa said that I could. The only reason Tulsa came into the picture was that Vince Carrilot was the defensive coordinator for Michigan State and they were recruiting me. During the recruiting process, he got the head coaching job at Tulsa, and started recruiting me. I had no idea where Tulsa was. I first thought it was in Texas and then confused it with Tulane, and thought it was in New Orleans. I finally looked it up and discovered that Tulsa was in Oklahoma.

I went to Tulsa for a visit and enjoyed it. It was during basketball season, and they always had good basketball teams. We went to a game that Saturday night and the place was packed. It was a vocal and exciting atmosphere. I thought to myself, *Man, if they're like this for basketball, they must really get into it for football.*

When I returned to South River, we were in our basketball season and I was ranting and raving to my teammates about Tulsa University and Bobby Smith. Bobby Smith was the basketball star at Tulsa. His nickname was "Bingo." He ended up getting drafted by the Cleveland Cavaliers and played a few years in the NBA. When I went to basketball practice, everything was Bobby Smith.... Bingo Smith... Bingo Smith from the corner.... Bingo Smith from the side.... Bingo

Smith from the top. The guys said, "Who the hell's Bingo Smith?" I tried to explain and I guess it was pretty obvious that I was kind of infatuated with The University of Tulsa.

We had talked about baseball during my visit to Tulsa and they told me that I could play baseball as well as football. At the same time, Nebraska was hot on me. Through the process of elimination, those were the final schools that I was interested in.

Nebraska really thought it had me. There were four guys in the state that year that they were targeting. All four of us were All State. One was Rich Glover, an all America who won the Outland Trophy during his stay in Nebraska. The other was Daryl Griffith, a big tackle. The third guy was a running back named Charlie Hinton. He had to go to junior college first before he would be eligible to get into Nebraska. I was the fourth guy. I was the final piece in their plan, which would give them a grand slam in New Jersey. They thought it was a no-brainer.

Kiffen was in town visiting and took us out to Highland Park Steak House for dinner. The only restaurant I'd been to before was Coffaro's in South River, a pizza joint. We never went out to dinner. There were seven kids. You don't take seven kids out to dinner.

This was all new to me. I can remember it like it was yesterday. I didn't know how to butter the bread or which fork to use and my mom was simply in awe. She was so happy to be taken out to dinner. We listened to Kiffen's pitch and I was swaying. This was big time football and he was talking about Sugar Bowls, Orange Bowls, and it got kind of exciting. After dinner he dropped us off at the house and stayed in a hotel because I was going to make my decision the next day.

By that time, I had already made another visit to Tulsa. I came back more impressed than ever. When I made my choice between

Nebraska and Tulsa, it shocked everyone, including my parents and my brothers and sisters. I chose Tulsa over Nebraska, mainly because of the opportunity to play football and baseball.

Shortly after I signed with Tulsa, its basketball team played in the NIT. The told me I was going to be invited. I never heard from them. I guess I signed too soon. As I think back on it, I picked Tulsa because I could play football and baseball but I think the thing that really sold me on them was that I loved their basketball team and Bingo Smith. Go figure, I was just 18 years old.

TULSA

CHAPTER EIGHT
★★★★★

I was excited about going to Tulsa. I had my bags packed about two weeks before the day we were going to leave, and my father was going to go with me. He was going to fly down and make sure I got settled, and then come back the next day.

We left on a Saturday morning and Tulsa was hot as heck. We got off the plane, and couldn't see anything but flat land. We took a cab to the campus and went to my dorm, La Fortune Hall, which was brand new. It was the first year they had the athletic dorm on campus, so everything was new. The rooms were great and we had our own cafeteria right in the dorm. My roommate, George Haynes, from Coffeyville, Kansas, hadn't made it in yet so my father stayed with me in the dorm room that night. While I was going through orientation the next day, Dad went out and walked around Tulsa. He was looking to see what kind of place it was. He became concerned that he didn't see many blacks there. Then, he got more concerned because when he finally did run into blacks, it was on the other side of town. You literally had to go across the tracks to get to the black area of town. He had also heard about racial issues and racial tension in town.

My recruiting class was really the first influx of black athletes into Tulsa. It had only been about three or four years since they had recruited the first black athlete. The group that came in with me caused a stir and a little concern to some of the people in Tulsa because it had only been a few years since the University of Tulsa was segregated.

Dad was supposed to leave the next day and ended up staying a week because he didn't feel comfortable leaving me there. When he finally left, the last thing I remember him saying before he got on that airplane was, "Son, are you sure you want to stay?"

My dad would never let me quit anything. If I was signed up and committed, I stuck it out. For him to say that, I knew he had to be worried but I said, "Yeah, Dad. I'm going to stick it out and see how it goes."

As it turned out, it was a tough adjustment. Here I was, coming from New Jersey and I was there with all these guys from Oklahoma and Texas. These guys were big dudes. I'd never seen people so big and fast, and such great athletes. I was like the odd ball. I was wearing my madras shirts, khaki pants, and saddle shoes. These guys wore jeans and cowboy boots, wide belts with big buckles on them....and these were the black guys. I was the butt of all the jokes. They were laughing at me, the way I talked, the things I ate, and, of course, the way I dressed. I knew once I got on the field, I was going to be equal because I was confident in my talents and abilities.

I knew what I was going up against. That year they brought in eight quarterbacks from around the country. We all had ambitions of being the quarterback for Tulsa. Of course, back then, freshman couldn't play on the varsity, so we played on the freshman team. I couldn't wait to get on the field, equalize things and try to get some respect from these guys, because they surely weren't respecting me off the field. It turned out to be the equalizer, because when we got on the field and they saw my athletic ability and talent, they gradually stopped messing with me. I started becoming one of them. And they wanted to hang around with me.

My freshman year I had a good season. Reid Johnson was my freshman coach. He later became a scout for the Cowboys and player personnel director for the Atlanta Falcons. He was a short, fiery kind of a guy. Out of the eight recruits trying out for quarterback, three moved to defense, one to running back and another to tight end. There were three of us left and I ended up beating them out for the starting position. I started at quarterback for all four of our freshman games.

We played our first home game in Skelly Stadium, which seated about 40,000. We never came close to filling it. Oklahoma University showed up with three bus loads of players. They were the biggest players I'd seen in my life. They had a fullback named A.G. Perryman from Texas who weighed about 246 pounds. We didn't have linemen in high school that big.

We ran a dive into the line on the first play. The second play we faked the dive, ran the option down the line of scrimmage and made the pitch off the defensive end. The defensive end was a guy named Leon Crosswhite, who ended up playing with the Detroit Lions as a fullback in the NFL. I stuck the ball in the fullback's stomach and pulled it out. I came down the line to run the option, pitched it at the last second, and Crosswhite decked me. It was the hardest I had ever been hit in my life. I had to decide then and there to get ready for more of this, because that's how it was going to be in college football, or get the heck back to New Jersey. The difference between high school and college ball was a rude awakening. The quality of athletes I was playing against was a major upgrade from high school. I had to make a decision to stay and play college football or give it up and concentrate on baseball. I made the decision I was going to stick it out. I shook off the hit and we ended up losing that game to OU, but we played them tough.

We went to Arkansas and played the Razorbacks. They had a running back named Jon Richardson and their quarterback was Joe Ferguson, who ended up having a great career with the Buffalo Bills. We beat them in Tulsa. Even though it was a freshman game, it was a big upset. We ended up finishing the freshman year 2-2. I was captain of the team and I had a good year as quarterback.

CHAPTER NINE
★★★★★

As soon as the freshman season ended, Vince Carilot, the varsity coach, called me in and said, "Hey, you've got a great chance to start as quarterback as a sophomore. But, you've got to make a commitment. I don't think you can play baseball, miss spring football practices and still have a chance to start." Basically, he was telling me, "If you want this, you've got to give up baseball." I was at a crossroads because baseball had been everything to me. I chose Tulsa so I could play baseball. The year before, the Tulsa baseball team had been to the College World Series. Their coach was Gene Shell. They had players being drafted by major league teams.

It was a tough decision. I talked to my father about it and his advice was, "If you do give up baseball and the football doesn't work out, you can always go back later and play baseball. Or, just continue to try to play both." But, I knew I couldn't play both because with my studies and the pressure of college football I couldn't do it. I made a decision. I gave up baseball and concentrated on football.

I went through spring training as quarterback. The guy ahead of me was John Dobbs, Glenn Dobbs' son. Glenn Dobbs was a legendary player for Tulsa and was now athletic director. When I was a freshman at Tulsa, his son was the incumbent quarterback. So, it was pretty much an uphill battle to beat him out. When spring ball ended, I was number two. When the season started, I didn't beat him out. I went into my sophomore season as the number two quarterback.

The first game of the year, we played at Arkansas and Dobbs started the game only to get hurt on the first series of plays. Arkansas was then a top-10 team. When Dobbs got hurt, I got thrown into the game. There were 50,000 people, all in red, yelling, "pig suey"…. and the skinny sophomore from New Jersey was playing quarterback against them. I was running for my life, and they ended up beating us, 56-7. I'm proud to say, however, I scored the touchdown that kept us from being shut out, even if it was a one-yard quarterback sneak. When we got to the one I was thinking, *Hey! I'm taking this one in. I'm getting my name in the paper.*

The fourth game into the regular season, I got the starting job, and we turned the season around. That was the only winning season I had at Tulsa. We finished 7-4 and tied with Memphis State for the Missouri Valley Conference title. There were no bowl offers and the 7-4 season was over but I had a nice year. Quarterbacking at Tulsa wasn't as glamorous as you might think. The line wasn't that good. You scrambled around a lot, fighting, and running for your life.

CHAPTER TEN
★★★★★

In high school football, the only black teammate I'd had was during my sophomore year. Carl Hill was a senior tight end. After he graduated, I was the only black on the team. I was the quarterback so nobody really saw any color and neither did I. I didn't notice anything black or white.

South River is a Polish town. Its nickname is Little Poland. Everyone there is a "Ski", like Scotty Skarzynski. I was about the only one whose last name didn't end in "Ski" so the guys on the team called me Drew-ski.

I dressed the way I did because of my environment. I dressed like the white kids that I was around. I didn't realize I was black until I got to Tulsa. At South River, most of the time I was the only black athlete. In basketball there was one other guy, and in baseball, there were no others. In our senior class at graduation time, there were two black girls and Drew-ski. Of course I knew I was black but all my mannerisms, the way I spoke, the things I was doing, were white-oriented.

Even my favorite foods were lasagna and pizza. Blacks are stereotyped and supposed to like fried chicken and collard greens. My big day was when my mom cooked lasagna. My favorite restaurant was Coffaro's Pizza. I was thinking, *I'm a white Italian with the name "Drew-ski"…. a white Italian, Polish guy.*

It was a rude awakening for me when I got to Tulsa, because other than being around my family, it was really the first time I had spent any significant time around black people, especially my own age, athletes just like me. It was an adjustment.

At Tulsa we bonded together because this was the first big number of black athletes they brought in. They recruited about twenty of us that year. We bonded together because we felt like we needed to stick together.

There was a U-Totem store down the street from our dorm and we would walk to the store. You could even see the store from our dorm; the stadium was to our right. We used to go to the store to get what we called the "Tulsa Steak", which was a honey bun and an RC Cola. I told the guys, "This is definitely an Oklahoma thing." I didn't even know what a honey bun was in New Jersey. One night we were walking back from the U-Totem and out of the bushes came these white guys. They started chasing us. We didn't know where they came from, if they were TU students or high school guys from town. About the same time, a pick-up truck screeched around the corner with its lights on bright and it was also was chasing us. We were flying down the street scared to death.

We got back to the dorm where we were safe but even though we had all experienced some racial discrimination in the past, none of us had ever known this kind of hatred. There was tension around the campus because a lot of people in the city were upset that Tulsa University had brought in all of the black athletes. They were going to try to scare us and run us off. That entire freshman year, we went to the store in large groups. Instead of two or three of us, there'd be five, six or seven of us going at one time. Sometimes we'd take a baseball bat in case we were confronted or had to fight. I had never really experienced anything like it before.

The blacks stuck together because we had to. Gradually, however, we became more accepted in the community and *by* the community of Tulsa and the rest of the people on campus.

With the white teammates race was never a problem. We didn't have any cars and for us to go out and have a good time, we had to go to the north side, which was across the tracks where all the blacks lived. We didn't have transportation, so we would sit around and wait until the white guys would come in from hanging out. They would come in early around 10:00 or so, and we would borrow their cars and go to the north side and hang out. We had no problems with the white teammates accepting us or us accepting them, including the coaching staff, which was all white. The dorm was our sanctuary. We had a new athletic dorm and it was state of the art and it was our domain. We seldom ventured out other than to go to class, football practice, and occasionally to the north side. We spent a lot of time in the gym working out and just didn't go anywhere around campus. There were clubs on campus where students would hang out but we didn't. Sometimes, on weekends, the coaches let us use their cars. We would go to the north side or rent a hotel room and have our own parties.

There were only a couple of black women on campus and I did hook up with one of them. She was an electrical engineering major from Beaumont, Texas. I was so shy and introverted that I could hardly talk to a girl back then, so that romance didn't go very far.

CHAPTER ELEVEN

★★★★★

I had no girlfriends in high school. My mom made me go to the senior prom. She had to ask the girl if she would go with me, because I was too shy to ask her.

I was as straight as an arrow and the only time I had a drink in high school was during my senior year on my 17th birthday. All my buddies picked me up and took me to a surprise party at a cheerleader's house. They said, "Come on, you're going with us," and they put me in the back seat of the car, popped open a beer and told me to drink it.

I said, "I'm not drinking that stuff. No way! No way!" They eventually made me drink a beer and that was the first alcohol I'd ever had in my life.

The whole first semester at Tulsa, I was awed by these big guys my age because they looked like grown men. During our first meal in the dorm, one guy was getting foil and wrapping up food. I asked him, "What are you going to do with that?"

He said. "Well, I've got my kids in the car. I'm going to take some food out to them."

I said, "What?" He had two kids and was the same age as me. He had a wife and two kids in the car and the kids weren't babies. I was thinking, *Damn, I haven't even had sex and this guy's got two kids.*

I was a virgin through high school. I had a girlfriend, but we never did anything (remember, my mom had to ask her out for me). The guy with the kids was named Arthur Calloway and he ended up starting at defensive back. He lives in Dallas now and is a good friend. His kids, of course, have kids now.

I didn't have a drink the first semester at Tulsa despite teammates trying to get me to try alcohol. They were drinking Mad Dog 20/20 and Boone's Farm wine.

The second semester they finally got me! After a tag football game in the parking lot, we went in the dorm and they decided to make Drew have a drink. I gave in and started drinking Boone's Farm. My God, what did they do that for? All of a sudden I was drunk for the first time in my life. I was also obnoxious, running my mouth and talking noise. We went back to the parking lot and started playing our game again. I threw a pass to Ed White, from Dangerfield, Texas. He was a big fullback, 5'11", 235 pounds, who was later drafted by the Denver Broncos. I threw him the ball, on the final play of the game and he dropped it. I wouldn't let it go. We got back to the dorm and I was still buzzing, still a little drunk. I said, "Damn, Ed, you cost us the game." I was ragging him and just playing, but Ed was mad. He had his back turned to me, and I attacked him. He turned around and knocked me silly. I went flying back into the air conditioner, and as I hit it, I just slid down.

The guys said, "Man, we should never give this guy a drink anymore."

They did get me drunk a couple of weeks later or I should say, I got myself drunk. Again it was Boone's Farm wine and my roommate, George Haynes and I, decided to visit one of the girl's dorms. The wine gave me enough nerve to talk to Cheryl Arbuckle, from Beaumont. However, it wasn't a normal conversation because I was loud and obnoxious. The dorm was the Lottie Jane Mabee Hall, and the dorm mother always sat out in front. I had to take George with me because I wasn't that bold. We called Cheryl and she came down from her room to visit with us in the lobby. She said, "Man, this guy's finally talking." But it was the alcohol talking, not me.

Visiting hours were over and everyone except the residents was supposed to leave, but I wasn't going anywhere. The next thing I knew, I was bad-mouthing, talking trash to the house mother and telling her, "I'm not going, I'm not leaving the dorm." I was yelling, using some cuss words, trying to get back where the girl's rooms were. I wasn't going to let Cheryl go. I was going to follow her to her room. I ended up getting thrown out of the dorm.

The guys said, "We're sorry we ever gave you a drink, man." George finally dragged me out of there and put me in bed.

I got up the next morning asking, "What happened, what did I do?"

George said, "Man, you better hope you don't get suspended."

Fortunately for me the incident was never reported to school officials and other than making a fool of myself there were no consequences.

We had a great bond between the black athletes. We had to stick together and we did. George Haynes and I are still close. A lot of the guys live down here in Texas, but to tell you the truth, not many stayed in Tulsa. George did, because his only option was to go back to Coffeyville, Kansas. Tulsa was an upgrade for him.

CHAPTER TWELVE

★★★★★

After the sophomore season of 7-4, it was pretty much downhill. The last two years, I don't even remember our record, except that they were losing seasons. Our only claim to fame came during my junior year when we played the University of Arkansas in Fayetteville. The Razorbacks were again a top 10-ranked team and we upset them 21-20. I scored a touchdown in that game.

After I made the commitment to football, I had professional football aspirations, and I knew I wasn't going to be a pro quarterback. It didn't have anything to do with being black, even though there weren't that many black quarterbacks getting drafted or getting opportunities in the NFL. I wasn't going to be a pro quarterback because I knew I didn't have the skills. I had to find another position.

After my sophomore year, Coach Carilot resigned because of pressure from the NCAA. We were being investigated and were hit with probation. We ended up on probation my junior and senior years. Carilot resigned to try to ease some of the penalties. It was all about recruiting violations. We had one booster who gave guys money.

Others tried to recruit Kenny Garrett, who was playing at NEO Junior College and most of the recruiting scandal related to the recruiting effort to get him. They offered him the world and the NCAA found out about it.

After Coach Carilot resigned, Tulsa hired Coach Claude "Hoot" Gibson. Most of his coaching experience was at the professional level. He had been an outstanding back for the Oakland Raiders. He was young, good-looking, had a wife and a couple of kids. We gravitated toward him because he could relate to us. I went through spring ball at quarterback. They had brought in three junior college quarterbacks and one of them was pushing me for the starting job.

I ended up finishing spring ball as the number one guy. But after the spring ended, I went to the coach and said, "Hey, you've got a pretty good quarterback. What would you think if I moved to wide receiver?"

He wasn't going to listen to that. He said, "Yeah, they're pretty good, but they're not tested. You've played a year as quarterback. You've got a year invested in that and my first season here I want to go with someone more established."

He wasn't going to move me to wide receiver, initially, but I kept selling myself and I kept asking. Just before the start of fall practice, he said. "O.K.," and he moved me to wide receiver.

Boy, that was an awakening. I was getting in shape to play quarterback, not to be wide receiver. In assigning me to wide receiver, it moved Ray Rhodes, who became a head coach and defensive coordinator in the NFL, from wide receiver to running back. You didn't want to play running back at Tulsa because it's like suicide. Rhodes was only about 175 pounds. He was a good runner and had ability, but he wasn't going to run over anybody. Ray was always mad at me because he had to move from wide receiver and get beat up at running back.

Going to those first practices as wide receiver was a shock because I was doing a lot of running now. It was 100 degrees in Tulsa. It was more of a dry heat, but 100 degrees is 100 degrees and I was down to about 150 pounds.

If I were going to be a professional football player, it was definitely going to be as a wide receiver. It wasn't going to be on defense because I wasn't keen on hitting people and sticking my head in there.

I played my junior year as wide receiver and I think I caught 22 passes the whole season. We had a terrible year. Todd Starks ended up being the starting quarterback. We had that one game where we played totally out of our heads, totally out of our realm and beat Arkansas in Fayetteville 21-20. Todd was the *Sports Illustrated* college football Player Of The Week. It was the first time anybody had even noticed that we were in Tulsa. When we got back to campus, there were even some people there to greet our bus. That was the first time that had ever happened.

Tulsa football wasn't well accepted in the area. People would say, "It's just those TU guys." That's how they referred to us. It was hard to find an article on us in the *Tulsa World* newspaper. It was all OU on the front page every week.

CHAPTER THIRTEEN
★★★★★

Things got better socially as time went on. We started hanging out in facilities around campus with white football players. We were more accepted and didn't have to go to the store in groups. There were no more incidents of being chased or any racial taunts, only two real tough years of football.

During my sophomore year, I met the girl that I married. She was a senior at Bishop Kelly High School. They had a college day and were taking their seniors to the Tulsa campus to show them around. My roommate, George, and I were walking across campus. And since there weren't many black women there, we noticed these two high school girls. We thought, *Whoa!* And went over and started rapping to them. They thought it was cool that college guys talked to them. One thing led to another and we got their phone numbers. There was a dance on campus and we asked them to come over for that.

The next thing I knew, I was dating Marsha Haynes. I had no idea that she was Marques Haynes' daughter. In the fifties and sixties Marques Haynes, the world's greatest dribbler, was probably the most famous basketball player in the world. He was a member of Abe Saperstein's Harlem Globetrotters, but Marsha had never mentioned that.

Marsha invited me to her house so I borrowed a car from one of the white guys and went out for a visit. I didn't go alone because I was still too shy. I took George with me. Her home was in the middle of Sand Springs, Oklahoma, but it seemed to us to be out in the country. When we pulled up to the gate, there was a huge house with a big iron fence, swimming pool, pool house, manicured lawn, and a driveway with a gate. On the brick columns on each side of the driveway, the script writing read *Marques Haynes*. I stopped the car. I said, "Marques Haynes? We must be at the wrong house." Then I put two and two together. Marsha Haynes,..... Marques Haynes, and said, "Man! He's her father!" I was ready to back out of there.

Marques wasn't there because he and his wife were divorced at the time. The first thing I asked Marsha was "Is your father Marques Haynes?"

She said, "Yeah."

I said, "Oh my God." I was awed. I was definitely in over my head. I'm from South River, New Jersey, and she was Marques Haynes' daughter, with private schooling and a Dodge Charger. I didn't even have a car. But we stayed there a couple of hours anyway.

The next time I went out there, Marques was outside riding a mower and cutting the grass. Marsha and I went in the house and were sitting in the living room, just talking. I had my baseball cap on. Marques came in and the first thing he ever said to me was, "You remove that hat in my house." As it turned out, Marques was great, but I really had problems with my mother-in-law.

CHAPTER FOURTEEN
★★★★★

I ended up catching 33 passes as a senior for a total of 55 receptions in two years at Tulsa. The blessing to the whole thing was that I had a great, receiver coach, Ted Plumb. Because of him, it was like a speed-reading course on the wide receiver position. I knew a little bit about running routes, and I could always catch, but he taught me how to run routes, how to have a feel for the defense, recognize defenses, and all of the little things that go along with the position. He ended up coaching in the pros with the Chicago Bears, Cardinals, Giants and Philadelphia. I was lucky that he was there, because after my senior season, it was time for the draft.

I wanted to play pro football and all of the scouts were coming to Tulsa to time guys in the 40 yard dash. Even though we didn't win many games, we had some good prospects. In fact, my junior year, we had two guys go in the second round. Ralph McGill, a defensive back, and Jean Barrett, both went to San Francisco. My senior year, Arthur Moore, a defensive end, also went to San Francisco. A couple of other players also got drafted. That was back when the NFL had 17 rounds of the draft and drafted about 452 players.

I worked out for a lot of scouts, but I'd always run the 40 in sweats because I didn't want the scouts to see my skinny legs. My 40 times were always around 4.6 and the criteria for receivers back then was 4.5. I wasn't that far off. The scouts were really there to look at the other guys but I would run and catch and work out for them as well.

Reid Johnson, who was scouting for the Dallas Cowboys, came to Tulsa. I don't know why but on the day he came, I decided to wear shorts. I say to this day, "That was my downfall."

People asked me, "Why didn't you get drafted?"

"I didn't get drafted because I wore shorts one day and the scouts saw my legs and thought, *This guy can never play football with those legs. As a matter of fact, how did he survive in college with those sticks?*"

I was in awe of guys who had nice calves. Mostly it was the white guys because blacks are more streamlined. You don't see many blacks with big calves. Even in the pros I never wore shorts. Hot as it was in training camp, I always had sweat pants on.

The first day of the draft came and went and I wasn't drafted. I was disappointed, because some of those scouts said, "You're fifth, sixth round material." But the fifth, and sixth rounds came and went, then so did the seventeen rounds. I was hurt. Halfway through the second day of the draft, I bought some Boone's Farm wine and started drinking, trying to cover up the frustration I felt. I got drunk sitting there on the couch with my new wife Marsha, trying to figure out what we were going to do.

Around 11:00 p.m. the night of the second day of the draft, the phone rang. Of course, you didn't have caller ID back then; you just answered to find out who was on the other end of the line. I answered and it was Bob Griffin from the Cowboys. He told me he couldn't believe I didn't get drafted. "We want to sign you," he said. "I'm at the Camelot Hotel. Can you come see me?"

I had a hangover from Boone's Farm, but I said, "Yeah, I'll be right there." So I got myself together, and got in Marques' old '54 Ford, which he had loaned us. When Marsha and I got married, her mom took the Charger away. The Ford had the gear shift on the steering column. It was Marques' pride and joy, probably the first car he bought when he got some money.

I drove to the Camelot Hotel and went to Griffin's room. He reiterated that he couldn't believe that I didn't get drafted. He gave me the spiel about how free agents who signed with the Cowboys always got an equal opportunity. He told me about Cliff Harris, Benny Barnes and Cornell Green. He told me they had changed Cornell from a basketball player to a football player, that Cliff Harris had come from a Division III school, and that Benny Barnes had come from Stanford and made the team. He offered a contract and said, "Do you want to sign?" I looked at the numbers — a three-year deal for $14,500 in the first year. He said, "If you sign now, I'll give you a signing bonus of $150." I wanted to sign because I wanted to be able tell everyone, "I didn't get drafted, but I'm going to be playing for the Cowboys." But I didn't sign then because of something F.A. Dry had told us before the draft.

Midway through our senior year at Tulsa, Coach Gibson was fired and F.A. Dry took over. Coach Dry talked to the seniors before the draft and said, "I hope you get drafted. But if you don't get drafted, one advantage you have as a free agent is that you get to pretty much pick where you want to go, the best situation for you." That was in the back of my mind when I met with Griffin and I didn't sign. I went back home, and the next day representatives from Green Bay and the Pittsburgh Steelers called. It was one of the Rooney's from Pittsburgh. He said he was in town and he asked me to meet him at the Holiday Inn north of Tulsa. He offered me more money than the Cowboys. He said the base would be around $20,000 and they would give me a $1500 signing bonus.

Green Bay never made an offer and it was probably because I didn't give them a chance. I didn't think I wanted to go to Green Bay. I had heard how cold it got up there and I didn't figure I could catch many passes with my hands in my pockets.

It was between Pittsburgh and Dallas and I ended up going with Dallas and their original offer for three reasons: Number one was Tom Landry. Number two, was their history of free agents making their roster. Number three was their proximity to Tulsa. I could get there quickly if I needed to. It's just a three-hour drive to Dallas from Tulsa.

CHAPTER FIFTEEN

★★★★★

Tulsa was now home and Marsha and I were living in an off-campus apartment. Because I was a married student athlete, my scholarship money increased from $15 to $75 a month. That was one reason we got married, to get the big money. I found out that it didn't go very far when your rent is $120 a month.

When we got married, Marsha had finished high school but we decided to put her college on hold and she went to work. The University set her up with a job at a day care center.

I was having problems with my mother-in law. She didn't want me to marry her daughter. She didn't think I was good enough.

When my family arrived for the wedding she was very disrespectful. She didn't accept them or even acknowledge their presence. My mother and father weren't good enough either.

I didn't know that she was treating them badly until my brother-in-law told me. This was the day before the wedding. We had a bachelor party at my apartment the night before the wedding. I partied all night long and could hardly get up the next day. My oldest brother, Sam, was at the party and he was going be my best man. Because of the hangover and the fact that my future mother-in-law didn't think I was good enough, I said, "Sam, I ain't getting married, I can't do it."

Sam said, "You've gotta get married, they're all here." He made me get dressed and put the tux on.

Sam drove me to the wedding in Coach Gibson's secretary's car. She let me use her car that weekend because she knew I was getting married. We went down the hill to Marsha's house and we could see people starting to mingle for the wedding. I told him, "Stop the car. I'm not doing this. I'm getting out."

He said, "Man, I'll kick your butt. I don't care what you do tomorrow, but you're getting married today. You can do what you want to tomorrow, but you're not going to embarrass your mother and father."

I said, "I don't like the way they've been treated." It wasn't Marques; it was Marsha's mother, Marquetta. Marquetta didn't think I was good enough. She did not want me to marry her daughter and didn't like me at all. She called me, "That boy." My name now was, "That boy." As in "Don't bring that boy in here," or "Is that boy coming?"

We pulled up to the house and she had it laid out. She had a bridge built over the swimming pool and at the top of the bridge was a champagne fountain. Champagne and flowers were everywhere.

She had to do this because of her status in society. In spite of the fact that she didn't like me, if she was going to have her society people at the wedding, she had to have an extravagant party.

All my teammates came to the wedding. They had a great time, drinking champagne and eating expensive food. They said, "This is a party, baby! It's a great wedding, Drew." I didn't smile the whole time. I went through all the procedure, the vows and all that, but I was not a happy camper.

Marsha and I didn't hang around long. Our honeymoon was at the Quality Inn in Tulsa where we spent one night. We had to leave by check-out time because I didn't have enough money for two nights. My father gave me all of the money he had but the Hayneses didn't give us anything for a wedding present because they had spent so much money on the wedding.

The day after the wedding, we were back at my apartment on Seventh Street. I helped my family get to the airport for their trip back to Jersey. The next day, Monday, I went to work at a job Marques got me with the Sand Springs Road Department. I was called a surveyor's helper and carried a sledgehammer around with stakes. When they surveyed the land I'd hammer in the stakes. The surveyor would tell me "lower," and I'd hammer it in a little lower, or "That's too far. Pull it up more." I helped lay the road that is the highway between Tulsa and Sand Springs. I like to say that I'm responsible for that road.

It was about 100 degrees outside, I was making $2.75 an hour, and I couldn't quit. It was my senior year. I was working in the hot sun all day long, eating lunch under a tree.

After my first day on the job, we loaded up and went back to the headquarters. Marsha was supposed to pick me up there. Her parents were letting us use her mother's big Lincoln Continental and Marsha was driving that. I was waiting, looking at my watch. …. She was fifteen minutes late… thirty minutes late. We had just gotten married and she evidently was not anxious to see me. She finally came in an hour and a half later. I had worked eight hours and she was that late picking me up. I thought, *What the heck did I get into?*

When football started, I had to give up the surveying job so we were living on what Marsha made. The whole time her mother was calling because she had found out that Marsha was working the job at the day-care center. The job was on campus, four hours a day in the morning. When Marquetta found out about it, she wasn't going to let that happen. She was not going to have her daughter married to a man who was playing football while his wife worked.

She called the day-care center and had them fire Marsha. Marsha came home crying and devastated. Marsha's mother was not going to let up. She had her sister, her brothers, and all of Marsha's aunts and uncles call to tell me, "You're not a man to have your wife work while you're playing ball." Marques was not in on this; it was Marsha's mother leading the charge. She forced Marsha to make a decision, either them or me. She went with me and that severed their relationship and caused a lot of hard feelings. I could never understand it because I wasn't a bad guy; I just never got a chance to prove it.

I told the coach my predicament. He didn't give me any money, but did hook me up with a student loan. I got a $1,500 loan, which carried us through the football season. I did, however, do one real dumb thing with some of the money. I went out and bought a full-length leather coat. I had seen the movie *Super Fly* and I guess it had some influence on me. I hardly had any pants or shirts to wear, but I had a leather coat. I bought the coat, took Marsha out to dinner, and we saved the rest of the money to carry us through the semester. I figured that I was going to get drafted in February, during the second semester, and would get some bonus money.

The student loan carried us through and Marsha didn't have to work. She took a couple of courses at the university but the whole time, her mother was relentless.

CHAPTER SIXTEEN
★★★★★

A few weeks after I signed, the Cowboys held a mini-camp for rookies in Dallas. I thought I was pretty special until I got down there and saw all the other rookies. There were 100 there, only seventeen were draft choices. The other 83 were free agents like me. They have restrictions now because of the salary cap and can only bring 80 players to training camp. Back then you could bring as many as you wanted. The Cowboys' philosophy was to "throw a lot on the wall and see what would stick", so they brought in as many free agents as they could handle. My roommate was Golden Richards, a second round draft pick. We stayed at the Hilton Hotel on Central Expressway. I thought Golden was a little weird and didn't gravitate toward him right away. There was another receiver, Zach Rogers, from Norfolk State. He didn't have a roommate, so I ended up leaving Golden and rooming with him.

The number one thing I noticed at the mini camp was that I had to work on my strength. When the mini camp ended and I went back to Tulsa and started living in the weight room.

At the end of March the Cowboys called and invited me to another mini camp for veterans. The Cowboys were the first to start the mini-camp concept. They held a camp at the end of each month.

When they brought the veterans in they also brought in selected rookies. They invited all of the draft choices and brought me back. I was on the practice field with Roger Staubach and Craig Morton, running routes. There were also some rookie quarterbacks Doug Sloan and Dan Werner, a 6-4 guy from Michigan State with a good arm. I snagged all of the passes from the rookies like I had always done in college.

When I ran routes for the veterans, the results were different. Roger was bringing it, Craig Morton was bringing it, and Jack Concannon was bringing it and I was dropping passes left and right. It wasn't a hand problem; it was strength problem. Once that ball hit my hands, I didn't have the strength to hold it. Their passes were coming harder than any balls I'd ever caught. And with a tight spiral.

After that mini camp I thought, *Oh my God, I'm in trouble.* I went to Tulsa and went to work in the weight room, because I knew what it took to catch now. I had to strengthen my hands, my wrists, and my upper body so I started pumping iron.

I was surprised when they called me back and invited me to the next mini-camp. The camp was mostly veterans and I had definitely improved my catching. I wasn't dropping anything. I had put a lot of time in, worked my butt off since the April camp and I was getting noticed. Coaches were watching movement, how you ran the route, and your knowledge. Even though I'd only played receiver for two years, my blessing was Ted Plumb, the receiver coach at Tulsa. He taught me how to run routes, so I was a little more advanced than some of the guys. Golden had speed and could make good cuts but I had fluidness. I could run that post corner, a sideline takeoff and I think I looked pretty good.

I went back to Tulsa and finished the school year. I was fifteen hours short so I didn't graduate on time. At the end of May they invited me back to their last mini-camp before training camp.

When Gil Brandt called me to come down to the mini camp, he said, "It would be in your best interest to move to Dallas and work out here on a regular basis." That was great with me and I was gone. Marsha's mother had helped her get a Volkswagen, but if she ever caught me driving it she was on my butt. We didn't have that much, but we packed everything we owned in the Volkswagen and moved to Dallas.

The Cowboys set us up with an apartment next door to the practice field. They found it but they didn't help pay for it. We were there about a week before the mini-camp and I thought, *How am I going to pay for this apartment? I don't have any money.* The Cowboys hooked me up with a job at Merchant's Van Lines on Irving Boulevard. My job was to load trucks. We loaded everything from refrigerators and TV's to furniture and one day we even loaded caskets. It was only a part-time job and I worked in the middle of the afternoon for about ten dollars an hour. I guess they had to pay that much back then to get people to load caskets. It was 100 degrees outside and inside the trucks it was 120-130 degrees. I was working out in the morning at the practice field and then going to work at Merchant's in the afternoon. I would get off at five or six o'clock, come home, eat, and go back to the practice field to work out again.

Roger seemed to like me. When the May mini camp ended most of the veterans left town to go on vacations with their families before training camp. Training camp was to start in the middle of July.

This particular summer, however, Roger didn't go on vacation. He came to the practice facility every day. I would be there and most mornings, he and I would be the only two guys on the field. He ran me relentlessly but it helped me learn to catch his passes and get used to the NFL game. He taught me all of the routes so I would already know them when I got my play book.

One day Roger said, "Man, you look kind of beat and tired."

I said, "Yeah, every morning I leave here and go to Merchant's Van Lines to load some trucks."

He said, "What? Let me see what I can do."

He went to the Cowboys and told them, "This guy is showing something. He's got a great work ethic. He's out here every day and has some ability." Roger actually told Gil Brandt, "I think he's got a chance to make this team."

The Cowboys called me the next day and said, "Hey, we heard you're working good and we appreciate that. Roger said you're looking good out there and that you've got a chance to make the team. We're going to give you some money so you don't have to load those trucks." Brandt gave me $500. Back then, that was a lot of money. I was able to pay rent for another month while I was in training camp, and Marsha was able to stay there until I started getting per diem money.

After that I was at practice 24/7, all day every day, and Roger was always there. It was a big thrill for me and I was trippin'. I was working out with Roger Staubach at the Dallas Cowboys practice facility with a Dallas Cowboys T-shirt on. I was sitting in the locker room with Mel Renfro and Calvin Hill.

I thought about home and figured that no one back there even knew this was happening. I didn't get drafted and they probably thought I had dropped off the radar screen. However, I started feeling good about my chances of making the team. After all, the Cowboys gave me that extra money and they were probably going to give me a longer look at training camp. I worked out that whole month of June and part of July with Roger.

Just before the rookies were to report to training camp, we got some money. You were able to fly on student stand-by, dirt-cheap back then, so Marsha and I flew to Jersey. I sat down and talked with my brother Sam who had been to the training camp with Cincinnati Bengals as a rookie. He knew about the training camp process and told me what to expect. I worked out in Jersey in the heat and humidity. It was good for me, because now I was heading to Thousand Oaks where the air was light and I would be able to run all day. I was in tremendous shape, but my brother told me, "I don't care how good of shape you're in, it's still not going to be enough."

GLORY DAYS

CHAPTER SEVENTEEN
★★★★★

As the plane landed in California all I could think was, *I'm going to make this team.* A representative from the Cowboys met me and I recognized him because he had a Cowboys T-shirt on. I guess I was expecting some kind of grand welcome and was a little disappointed when the first thing he said was, "Get your luggage and get on the bus over there. We've got to wait for a few more flights to come in." We waited two hours before they filled the bus up and then we headed for Thousand Oaks.

It was my first time in California and I thought it was the most beautiful place I'd ever seen. The weather, the mountains, and the ocean were magnificent. I remember coming up Highway 405, up the hill past Westwood and downtown L.A. We were chugging along in that bus with mountains on each side and I had never seen anything like it. We got to the top of the hill and could see the whole valley. It was awesome!

There were about 20 of us on the bus and we stopped at a Howard Johnson's to eat. We then went to the dorm at Cal Lutheran

College and checked into our rooms. They were suites with two rooms on each side, separated in the middle by closets and bathroom. There were three of us on each side. The beds were small and Harvey Martin's feet hung off the bed. If he turned in the bed, he'd fall off. Harvey, Bill Pipp, and I were on one side. James Ray, a quarterback from Georgia Tech that they were trying to turn into a safety, and two other guys were on the other side.

We had a team meeting that night and the next day we were on the practice field. The first thing that came to my mind after the first couple of drills was what my brother said: "Whatever shape you're in, it ain't gonna be enough." He was so right. The whole first week of training camp was just rookies. There were a hundred of us and Coach Landry was going to weed us out. He made this part of training tougher than you can imagine. He wanted to see if we could handle it, not only physically but mentally. How much could we take? Could we learn the system? How much could we absorb before we were overloaded and it got too complicated?

The practices were grueling, three and a half hours long, twice a day. When the end of that week came Landry had to release some guys. Most of those that got cut were glad to go.

On our side of the suite, all three of us had survived. Every morning one of the trainers would knock on your door. When you opened the door, the trainers would say, "Rise and shine." If they lingered you knew something was up, because then they were going to call somebody's name, "So and so, Landry wants to see you. Bring your play book." That's when you knew it was over.

As they came down the hall one morning, Harvey and I were thinking, *Oh, God! What's our fate going to be? Is it going to be our turn?* We survived but they cut two guys next door.

We got back to the room after breakfast. We had a little dead time between breakfast and the first practice. We were excited because the trainer had been there and didn't get us. Bill Pipp, our other roommate, was a linebacker from Michigan. On the way back he stopped at the college bookstore and bought postcards. He was sitting there writing to his parents, " I survived another day." Before he could get "another day" written out, the phone rang and it was for him. Coach Landry wanted to see him and asked him to bring his play book. He got cut then and there, just like that, and he was one guy who didn't want to go. He started crying and it was hard to watch. I knew how he felt, because I think I would have cried, too.

Now the room was almost empty. There were only three of us left, Harvey and me on one side, and James Ray, still hanging, on the other side. Because our beds were together and there was nothing but a little floor separating us, I said, "Harvey, why don't you move into Bill Pipp's bed?"

He said, "No, why don't you move into that bed?" We were afraid to move because we thought it was jinxed.

"Why don't you move on the other side?"

"I ain't goin' over there."

We just stayed where we were and got through that first week.

The next week, here came the veterans, and these were the Cowboys.... Staubach, Reeves, Morton, Lilly, Hayes, and on and on. That first Sunday afternoon practice when they hit the field they were like clockwork. They were coming in and out of the huddle, breaking like they'd never left. I thought, *These guys know their stuff.* Back then, everyone played in the same system year in and year out. They were popping in and out of the huddle, and it looked like they were in mid-season form. All the rookies were thinking, *How are we ever going to catch up to this enough to even be considered for making the team.* There was no slowing down for the rookies. It was up to us to get on board and catch up to their pace. It meant constantly studying your play book and it was very complicated.

Our play books were like encyclopedias, thick with all kinds of information. I had never had so many assignments. With every running play, I had a blocking assignment. You'd think that the blocking assignment would just be to block the guy in front of you, but that wasn't the case. Sometimes you blocked the linebacker or the safety. And other times, you blocked the defensive end. I'd never done anything like that, so it was a process of trying to digest all of that information and still show some things athletically on the field. Coach Landry always said, "If you're going to make a mistake, at least make it full speed. Make something happen, and if you make a mistake, we'll correct the mistake. If you make a mistake and you still aren't making any plays, you're not doing anyone any good." I picked up the passing game well but had trouble with the running game and the blocking assignments. I picked up the passing game pretty easily because being a former quarterback, and having worked with Roger in Dallas before I got to training camp, I had an advantage. That really helped me, but I was still making mistakes, and I was scared because I didn't know when it was going to be my last mistake. Landry was working the veterans, too. He was putting us all through the wringer.

Thousand Oaks was a great place to train because of the weather and atmosphere out there. I couldn't believe the throngs of fans that would watch our practice. We had more fans watching us practice than I'd ever had watching my games at Tulsa. Fans were lined up and after workouts they'd want your autograph. When I look back it was a pretty cool experience. When you're there, your focus is on trying to make the team, not messing up, not making Coach Landry mad, and not making anyone else mad. You're trying to do what you've got to do to survive another day. It was a day-to-day thing and you never looked down the road. If it was Monday, you never looked to Friday; you looked to Tuesday. You dealt with Monday and hoped Tuesday would come. You dealt with Tuesday and hoped Wednesday would come. Every day Harvey and I would get out the playbook and our roster list of the veterans and the rookies and check off the names. That rookie list would be dwindling. We'd be in our own process of elimination from what we saw. We'd say, "That guy will never make it," or "I think we're in good shape with this guy." We were hoping that we could find a place in the mix somewhere.

They called Harvey in that second week. Defensive coordinator, Ernie Stautner had a "Come to Jesus" meeting with Harvey. He told Harvey, "You're too nice. You're never gonna make this team. You need to toughen up."

Harvey came back to the room and said, "Drew, I can't believe what they told me. But I'm gonna do it. I'm going to be transformed overnight from "Too Nice" to "Too Mean" Martin."

Overnight he transformed himself. He was still a great guy, a nice guy off the field, but when he got on the field he became a different person. Harvey was from Dallas and the Cowboys had drafted him in the third round. He wanted to be a Cowboy more than anything so he adjusted and changed. It was all of a sudden and I watched the transformation because I was there in the dorm with him. Once we broke camp and moved to Dallas, rookies had to stay in hotels, and Harvey was still my roommate.

We were trying to learn the system and the plays. At the same time, we were trying to do all we could with our physical abilities.

Coach Landry's play book wasn't easy. Everything about it was different. On every other football team I had ever played on, plays to the right on offense were even numbered plays and plays to the left were odd numbered. With Coach Landry, however, it was the opposite. You ran a Toss 37 Switch to the right instead of to the left. It took a while to get all of that stuff down, not to mention the other terminology that was totally new to most of the rookies. The snap count, how we lined up, and the motion plays were all different. He did these things to keep the opposing defenses off balance. When they heard an audible, "Red 37 – Red 37", the defense would think it was going to go to the offense left and the defense right. But, of course, it was going the opposite way.

He did all of those things to confuse the defense, and make the defense think. It almost made me believe that he didn't think defensive guys were very smart.

While we were in training camp the rookies always had to do things for the veterans. We had to get their beer, their ice, bring their food to them, or go to the store for them. My guy was Bob Hayes. Bob said, "Drew, you don't do nothin' for nobody else but me. If anybody asks you, you tell them you're Bob's guy."

I said, "Okay. That's cool." I was in awe of Bob Hayes. Bob was helping me on the field and telling me my assignments. I think a lot if it had to do with the fact that I was from New Jersey. Bob's wife at the time was from New Jersey, just one town over from where I grew up. Because of that, he might have had a special feeling for me.

One Sunday afternoon we had the day off and all of the rookies were in our room. We were lying around on the beds, talking and telling stories about our college days, just passing time until dinner time. Out of the blue, Bob Hayes opened the door. He looked around, pointed to me and said, "Rookie, you come with me. Put your shoes on and come with me."

I asked, "Where are we going?" I quickly put on my tennis shoes.

He said, "Don't worry about it, you just come with me." All the other guys were in awe because Bob Hayes had called me out. I followed Bob down the hall of the dorm, down the steps, and out the door. He said, "Get in the back seat." In the back seat was this girl, and there was a girl in front, driving. Bob jumped up front with the driver and I got in the back seat with the other girl. As soon as I got in the car, she planted a kiss on me and I almost died right there. All the guys were looking out the window as I drove off with Bob Hayes and those girls.

We ended up going to the Howard Johnson's where they had a suite. There were two other veteran players there and each had a girl. I wasn't there long before I was ready to go back. I was afraid I'd miss a meeting that night. I thought, *I hope this doesn't blow it for me and keep me from making the team.*

I finally got back and all the guys wanted to know what happened. I didn't tell them much because I was uncomfortable with the whole thing. I didn't miss the meeting and after that, because of Bob, I was pretty well accepted by the veteran players.

CHAPTER EIGHTEEN
★★★★★

After the first week of practice with the veterans, we had what they call the CLC scrimmage. CLC stood for Cal Lutheran College, where we trained. The CLC scrimmage was a big deal for the people in the area and it was a big deal for Cowboys fans. We would have a walk-through in the morning and in the afternoon we'd have the scrimmage. The place would be packed. It was a small stadium; they were a Division III school for football so the stadium wasn't that big. The sidelines would be packed five to ten people deep and it was a tremendous atmosphere.

I finally got some game time in the scrimmage, and the quarterback threw me a quick sideline pass. I bobbled and skipped out of bounds, but it was a good catch and I felt pretty good about it. What really turned things for me, however, was a running play. It was a "Toss 36 Switch" and my job was to do a crack-back block. Doug Dennison was running the sweep, I came in, saw the safety react and I annihilated him, probably because he wasn't looking. I hit him up under the shoulder pads. He went spinning and fell. Dennison went off me for a big gain. The coaches were hootin' and hollerin'. Our people were slapping me five, but I was thinking it wasn't that big of a deal.

We got through the scrimmage, and a lot of fans were coming down from the stands and mobbing the players. This was my first real experience of people wanting me to sign an autograph. The veterans signed a few autographs and then split because this was Saturday and they knew we had Saturday night off. The rookies, however, loved it and stayed until dark signing autographs.

The next time we came together as a team was Sunday night and after we filed into the meeting room, Coach Landry started critiquing the scrimmage and pointing out people that played well. He said, "Drew Pearson made a good block and that's what we want from our wide receivers. That's what you've got to do to make this football team." After that, in the Monday morning practice, I started getting more reps. I was thrown into the mix with the veterans and wasn't just running plays with the rookies. They were calling my number a little more and I think they started giving me a hard look.

Our first exhibition game was at night against the LA Rams in the Los Angeles Coliseum. I hadn't played any night games in high school and only a few in college. We filed on the bus and made our trek to LA from Thousand Oaks and as we pulled up to the coliseum, I thought, *Whoa, this is cool. Pro football.* We got off the bus and went down the tunnel. The fans were yelling, wanting our autographs. They were yelling for Lilly, Hayes, Staubach, and all the big names. We finally made it to the locker room, and I couldn't believe I was dressing with these guys and getting ready to play a professional football game.

While we were riding to the coliseum, the coach told me that I would be first in line to return punts. Reid Johnson, who was my freshman coach in college, was now working for the Cowboys as a scout. Since he knew me, he convinced Coach Landry that I could handle punt returns. He told Coach Landry that I had the best hands on the team and that I could catch anything. I was thinking about this the whole bus ride. My brother had come to town for the game. I told him, and he said, "Don't worry about it. You'll be fine." I thought my brother would be in the stands, but I looked around and he was standing on the sidelines hanging out right behind the Cowboys bench. How he got there, I'll never know.

The Rams didn't punt the football until late in the second quarter. I stood there at the 50-yard line at the LA Coliseum looking for a friendly face in the stands; I looked at Coach Landry, the Cowboys, and the Rams on the other side. They finally punted the ball and I got right under it. It hit me in the shoulder pads and slithered right through and bounced on the ground. The Rams jumped on it and I went to one knee and put my head in my hands. I turned to the left to look over to the sidelines and I could see Coach Landry over there just shaking his head. I thought, *Oh, man, that's it. I probably won't get another chance.* When I went to the sidelines no one spoke to me. It was like I had a disease because everyone moved away from me. They figured, *He's gone. No sense being friends with him. He won't be around much longer.* No one talked to me and I was sick. I was praying that I would get another chance.

They punted again in the third quarter. Coach Landry threw me out there and I got my other chance. It was almost the same situation. The Rams were back in their territory and I was on the 50. The guy punted a boomer, driving me back a little and I caught it on our 40. I took it up field, shook the first guy and went to the sideline, picking up the blockers. The next thing I knew, I was streaking down the sideline.

What was funny was that while I was trying to outrun the Ram's defense, my brother was running down the sideline with me. It was like back in South River when we were running from the cops. Their punter knocked me out of bounds on the one-yard line and the first guy that picked me up was my brother.

That play helped me redeem the fumble and gave me another shot and another day to play in the NFL. I'd made a big play, and I was going to get a longer look. We went back to training camp, and I started getting more looks, more reps, and more opportunities.

We played the Miami Dolphins in my first game at Texas Stadium as a Cowboy. We were losing and were lackluster making the trip from Thousand Oaks. We were home and all we were thinking about was being with our families, so we might have lost some focus early in the game. Coach Landry talked to us at half time and said. "We need to pick it up. We need a spark. We need to get going."

I was returning kickoffs and starting the second half. They kicked off to us. I took it, found a lane, took it down the sideline past the Cowboys bench, and returned it 53 yards into their territory. It pumped the fans and they were cheering again. Our players were pumped up, beating me as I went to the bench. We had played two exhibition games, and I'd made two big plays. Again, I'd lived to play another day.

The next exhibition, we went to Houston and played the Oilers in the Astrodome. The fourth quarter started and I was a frustrated because I hadn't played the entire game. I was concerned because I knew cut-down time was coming and Golden Richards had gotten a lot of time in the game. They finally put me in about half way through the fourth quarter. Craig Morton called me in on a route where I went in motion but not all the way across to the tight end. I cut up field before

I got to the tight end and ran a post pattern. Craig threw me the ball. It laid out there where I had to reach with my right hand, tip it back into my body, and make the catch. It was about a 50-yard gain. I made another play. I had limited opportunity, but I made another play. I lived to play another day.

When we broke camp for our final exhibition game, I knew I wasn't going to play much because Landry's philosophy for the last preseason game was to let the veterans play at least three quarters. He wanted them to be able to start the game, play the first half, and get the feel of going in at half-time and having to come back out and play another quarter. The veterans played most of the game and he threw us rookies in at the end. I caught a pass or two, but didn't really make anything happen.

Now came the real anxiety, of who makes it, and who doesn't make it. Harvey and I were going over the roster in our playbook and the whole time we were crossing off names. You could see that the list had really dwindled. There were only a few of us left. We were thinking, "Well, we don't really need him. He could go." We were cutting everybody but ourselves, of course.

Harvey called me that Monday evening after the Saturday exhibition game, and said, "Hey man, turn to Channel 5. They're getting ready to announce the rookies that made the team." I turned to Channel 5 and the sportscaster came on announcing the rookies. He didn't do it by just throwing up all of the names of those that made it up on the screen. He announced them one at a time - Harvey Martin, Golden Richards, Bruce Walton. Then he said, "Drew Pearson."

I said, "Oh my God. I made it!" I couldn't believe it.

Harvey called me back, "We made it homeboy!"

I said, "Yeah, yeah. I've gotta go. I've gotta make some phone calls."

I called home to all my friends and family and they were in shock. They couldn't believe it, either. They were ecstatic. You could hear everyone cheering in the background. "Drew made it. Drew made the Cowboys!"

After you had made it, the real challenge was to be part of the traveling team. They kept 47 players on the traveling team and another six on the taxi squad. The guys on the taxi squad didn't go to the away games. Coach Landry didn't even let you stand on the sidelines at the home games if you weren't suited up. I thought, *Man, I've got to be playing. I can't be making the team and not going to the games.* It was all about what you could do, what your value was to the team. If you're playing wide receiver and only catching passes, you're not that valuable. But if you're playing wide receiver and you're also on special teams, you have a little more value. I was on the kick-off coverage team, the punt return team and the kick-off return team, so that kind of gave me an edge over Golden Richards. Golden mainly returned punts but not kick-offs and wasn't on the kick-off team. I made the traveling team and Golden stayed home. Nothing against Golden, but that was a moral victory for me. He was the number two-draft choice; I was the free agent. He got the big signing bonus; I got $150.

I backed up Otto Stowe and Mike Montgomery at wide receiver when the 1973 season opened. Stowe was a big reason I was able to make the Cowboy team. I had only played wide receiver for two years, and when I got to the pros, my first wide receiver coach was Mike Ditka. Ditka had just retired and was now in his first year as coach for the Cowboys. He may have been the wide receiver coach but he knew nothing about wide receivers. He was a Hall of Fame tight end and could teach all the tight ends what to do, but he knew zero about wide receivers. He couldn't teach me how to get off the line, how to run a pass route, how to get in the breaks, how to come out of the breaks, how to run that sideline take-off, or how to make those moves and not stutter your steps too much. He never taught me any of that. I learned all that from watching Stowe, and Stowe learned it from playing three years behind Paul Warfield at Miami. In the off-season the Cowboys had traded Ron Sellers to Miami for Stowe. That did two things: It got Stowe who was a great receiver to Dallas and it freed up Sellers' number, No. 88.

Up to that point my number had been 13. I thought they were trying to write me off pretty quick. I hadn't seen too many guys wearing 13 and nobody really wanted it. When they gave it to me, I thought they might be trying to tell me something before I even got started. So, even after that scrimmage, when signing autographs, I would just sign "Drew Pearson." I wouldn't sign "Drew Pearson # 13", because if I made the team that certainly wasn't going to be my number.

Every day watching Otto run his pass routes, I tried to emulate him. I tried to run mine the same way he did because he was running the same way Warfield did. I knew this because I had studied Warfield. To me, he was the sweetest route runner that ever played the game. Because he was fluid, he could get deep, he could make the tough catch, and he could stop on a dime. I watched Otto who didn't know that he was teaching me by example. Even after I made the team and we were practicing, I was like a sponge, trying to gain all the knowledge I could about the position from Stowe. Ditka taught me my assignments but he didn't teach me how to carry out the assignments. He taught me how to carry out the blocking assignments. He usually said, "Go in there, take your position, and knock his head off!"

I'd say, "You know Mike, he might be about 260."

He'd say, "I don't care, just hit him!" But, he'd never told me anything about how to run a pass route. I learned all of that from Otto Stowe.

Otto was having a phenomenal year. He was catching balls, the tough catches, running beautiful routes, and blocking. The most surprising thing was the way he was blocking and coming after people. He set the precedent for being physical as a wide receiver and now we all had to block like that. We all had to be gung ho. That's what Coach Landry demanded. He always said, "You can't play wide receiver for me unless you can block." You had to be able to block first because we ran first and threw second. Blocking was important to all of us, but I even learned blocking techniques from watching Stowe.

I was returning punts and kick-offs and was on the kick-off coverage team. I really didn't do anything spectacular, but there was a lot of pressure because most of the games we played were in the afternoon. In Texas Stadium during the afternoons, part of the stadium was in the shade and part of it was in the sun. It was tough catching punts in Texas Stadium but after fumbling the punt in my first exhibition game in L.A., I didn't fumble anymore. I was trying to keep pace as a wide receiver and I stood third string behind Otto Stowe and Mike Montgomery.

In the eighth game we played Philadelphia in Philly. We ran a sweep to Calvin Hill and Calvin wasn't the most mobile or elusive type of runner. Otto was blocking the cornerback in front of him, using what we used to call the rooster block, where you engage the defensive back up high and try to occupy him. When you felt the running back coming, you would try to cut him at the last second. I guess Otto never felt Calvin coming because he was doing the rooster block and Calvin ended up getting tackled and fell on Otto's ankle. That same hard Veteran Stadium turf ruined a lot of players' careers. Calvin ended up breaking Otto's ankle and Otto was out for the year. The next week we played the New York Giants in the Yale Bowl. They were building the Meadowlands and the Giants were playing their home games in New Haven, Connecticut. Early in that game, Mike Montgomery pulled his hamstring, so he was out and I was in. That was the ninth game of my rookie year.

The next game, Otto and Mike were on the shelf and I was the only one left so I had to start. We played the Philadelphia Eagles at home. That week in practice, I was doing everything I could to give Coach Landry, my teammates and the quarterback confidence in me, and let them know I was ready to play. I worked and ran routes before practice and after practice. I wanted to show those guys that I was ready to play and that I could step in and do the job.

This was a Sunday before the Thanksgiving Day game. The whole game, I had one pass thrown to me. Coach Landry called my number in the second quarter. He called me on a "83 — 12-yard out." I caught it from Roger for nine yards and skipped out of bounds. I didn't even get hit. That was it. That's all he threw to me the whole game. What Coach Landry was trying to do was gradually get me acclimated to the game as a starter and get me used to playing four quarters. He didn't want to put pressure on me to be out there making plays. Plus, we were moving the ball and dominating the Eagles.

Four days later, we played the Miami Dolphins in Texas Stadium on Thanksgiving Day. What I remember most was that we lost the game, 14-7, on a beautiful sideline take-off by Paul Warfield. He was the master. He was so sweet. Some people just run pass routes, but Warfield was so graceful that it was just like poetry in motion. His steps, his leg kick, and his gait were incredible.

Most receivers, when they come off the field, rest, get Gatorade and sit there until it's their time to go back on the field. I was the type of player that liked to be involved with the game. If there was a good wide receiver on the other side, I watched him. I got my drink and was back on the sidelines, watching. I would anticipate a certain route might be coming because we were the scout team all week and I was Warfield in practice. I tried to run the sideline take-off on Mel to get him ready for it when it came in the game, and I could never beat Mel in practice. He jumped on it every time.

Late in the fourth quarter, Paul lined up to the left and Renfro came out on him. The clock was running down so Mel was a little off. He was in zone coverage, but if there was a man in his area, he had to cover him. Warfield came off the line with that high knee kick, a little stutter step. He took two steps to the sideline, did another step, and took it back inside Mel. Mel tried to spin and recover but Warfield was downfield and Bob Griese laid up a beautiful pass. That gave them the lead 14-7 and that was the ball game.

The other significant thing in the game was that I caught seven passes for 71 yards. All of a sudden, Coach Landry was going to me. He gradually eased me into it that first game and now he was going to find out what I could do. All of the passes I had caught were inside routes, "eighty-fours" and "sixteens." Eighty-four was the deep come back and sixteen was the deep turn-in, which later became my bread and butter route with Roger. I caught them; I took the licks and I had to go high to get a couple of them. I came down with the ball every time. From then on, the coaches, players, and of course, Roger, started having more confidence in me and I started spending even more time working with him before and after practice.

The final game of the regular season was against the St. Louis Cardinals in Busch Stadium, and it was a freezing day. It was that icy kind of cold with rain and sleet. It felt wet and there was snow all over the sidelines. It turned out to be the coming out game for Drew Pearson. I caught my first two touchdowns in the NFL. I caught five passes for 140 yards. The first touchdown was a post corner on Dwayne Crump. I took him to the post and brought it back to the corner. He slipped on the ice and I was able to catch it as Roger laid it in there perfect. I caught it just before I hit the back of the end zone and slid into the snow. It was like the old days growing up, playing slow motion football with your brothers in the snow. Later in the game, Roger called me on a post pattern and I beat Crump again. He hit me as I was catching the ball in the end zone. I got up and spiked the ball.

The pass that I remember more than anything was one I caught over the middle. Roger threw it high. I had to go up and get it. Hands, no shoulder; all hands. I snatched it and pulled it in, and as soon as I caught it, I got hit. I did a flip and came down with the ball and held it up. When you make a play like that for your quarterback, when you show your quarterback that you're going to go over the middle, do everything to make the catch or at least knock the ball away, and keep that defensive back from making the interception, then he's going to have more confidence in you than if he had hit you for a touchdown. He knows that you're going to make a play for him.

The next week we were going into the playoffs. Now I had a lot of confidence and Coach Landry and Roger had confidence in me. We played the Rams. Early in the first quarter Roger called me on a quick sideline route. I lined up in close to give myself some room on the sideline. I gave a little outside release, straightened it up and then drove to the sideline. Charlie Stukes was the cornerback. He was sitting there and by the time I broke it, I had separation. When I looked back, the ball was coming and Roger hit me about two yards into the end zone. I skipped along the end line, made sure I had my feet in bounds, and then did my spike.

I knew there were people watching back home on national TV. They might have missed my other touchdowns because the games were regional, but I was sure they'd see this one. It was probably freaking people out. "Is that Drew Pearson? This can't be Drew Pearson - the skinny legs, the little guy, no muscles – This can't be Drew Pearson."

I caught my first playoff touchdown, and that gave us the lead. We extended the lead to 17-0. It was exciting because of the playoff atmosphere in Texas Stadium. Everyone was buzzing and yelling. But the Rams came back to score a touchdown in the fourth quarter and cut our lead to 17-16. We were concerned. We had lost all of our momentum and the Rams were rolling. Our fans stopped yelling and cheering. Our next drive started inside our own 20-yard line after the Rams kicked off. We ran a running play to Calvin Hill up the middle for no gain; We ran a pass next. Roger got the ball, pass protection broke down, and Fred Dryer, who played *Hunter* in the TV show – a defensive end and a lot better football player than actor – sacked Roger. It was now third and 18. Coach Landry sent in a conservative play. He wanted to pick and punt. Maybe "Doomsday" could stop these guys; we could get the ball back, extend the lead, and move on to the next round of the playoffs. All we had to do was win two games to get to the Super Bowl, and during my rookie year, the Super Bowl was in Houston at Rice Stadium. It was a perfect scenario that was starting to unfold if we could just stay on track. It was Drew Pearson's perfect scenario for his rookie year — making the team third string, ending up starting, touchdowns in the final game, and a touchdown in a playoff game. It was third and 18 and Roger called off Coach Landry's play because he wanted to run something else. He said, "It's a two route play." He told Bob Hayes to line up on the right side and run a post pattern and stretch the defense. He told me to line up on the left side and run a post pattern down the other side of the field. The last thing Roger said when we broke the huddle was "Drew, I'm coming to you."

I thought, *Oh my God!* You don't think while it is happening, but when I look back, I think, *Man! I'm a rookie, 160 pounds, from Tulsa – first year salary $14,500, and a signing bonus of $150. What am I doing in this situation?*

I was in this playoff game and the Cowboys were counting on me to make a play. Sixty-five thousand people in the stands, millions watching on national TV, family, friends, everyone was watching. I came out of the huddle and lined up on the left side. Roger barked, "Hut one -- hut two." Hayes went flying downfield. When I came off the line of scrimmage, I noticed I was double covered. Eddie McMillan, a cornerback, was on the outside, and Steve Priest, a safety, was on the inside. They were bracketing me. Usually when a quarterback sees that double coverage, his read is away from you. He's supposed to go to the other side, but since we only had a two-man route, Roger was going to me anyway. I ran between those two guys. Both stepped in front of me and each thought he could make the interception. As they did, the ball zipped past them and they ended up colliding with each other. I caught the ball on the 50-yard line and there was no one there. I turned and ran and it was an 83-yard touchdown pass. I was so excited running into the end zone that I tried to do this little high-toed kick. It didn't come out too well and I think it looked kind of ugly. But it did blow the game open and we won.

The next week we played the Minnesota Vikings. Again, we

had the home field advantage at Texas Stadium. I didn't catch many balls in that game, didn't have many thrown to me. It was that way every time we played the Vikings, even in the Hail Mary game where I only had one ball thrown to me before that final drive.

The Vikings played the type of defense that kind of took me away. They rolled up to my side. The quarterback reads that and he's told through his progression to go somewhere else. We played the Vikings in that NFC Championship Game, and I didn't get many passes thrown. With all due respect, Roger had a bad game. What broke our back was his sideline pass to Bob Hayes. Bobby Bryant, the cornerback, picked it off and took it all the way back for a 63-yard touchdown. That broke the game open. We lost to the Minnesota Vikings 27-10. They went on to Houston and lost to Miami in the Super Bowl.

I was totally dumbfounded. Even though I'd gone through the whole process, mini-camps, working out before training camp, training camp, making the team, the season, starting the 10th game of my rookie year, catching my first touchdown, and playing in my first playoff game, I still wasn't tired. I wasn't burnt out. I was excited about playing and wanted to continue. I wanted to go on. I wanted one more game.

Marsha and I caught a plane on Monday and were in New Jersey by mid-afternoon. I had to go home. I had to be reassured that it was me and that I did all of those things. The way I got my reassurance was by the acceptance from the people of South River. "Aww, Drew Pearson." They were watching. They did know about it. "Drew Pearson, you played for the Cowboys on TV yesterday, and now your here." Marsha couldn't understand why we had to go so quick. She said, "Why do we have to go now?" I had to get home. I had to be reassured that I had made the team.

Harvey Martin, Billy Joe Dupree and I got jobs in that off-season, because we didn't make enough money to live on playing football. We worked every off-season. We worked for Cullum and Boren Sporting Goods, which was owned by the Zales Corporation. Now you have Oshman's and Academy, but back then it was Cullum and Boren. We went to them together to ask for a job. We wanted to work our way up through the Zales Corporation. We were into sporting goods. I knew more about sports than all of these guys — *all the sports.* Billy Joe was a football player and golfer. Harvey played football and that was it. They put me in the sporting goods equipment department. Harvey and I were in the North Park store. Billy Joe was in another store. Harvey sold shoes. Back then, you didn't pick out a shoe, grab a box, try it on, and ask the guy to go in the back and see if he had your size. You told the salesman what you wanted, he went back and got the shoe, and then he had to get down on that little stool with a shoehorn. Harvey would be down there trying to put shoes on customer and the sight was laughable.

When Harvey got down on that little stool, his legs stuck up higher than his shoulders, because Harvey was all legs. When Harvey stood, he was taller than anyone. When he sat, he was shorter than anyone. I used to say, "Harvey, you can reach over your shoulder and get your wallet out of your back pocket because your legs are so long."

Harvey said, "Homeboy, I don't know how much more of this I can take."

I said, "Harvey, we've gotta stick it out, man. We've gotta stick it out."

I played out my contract that rookie year. I hit all of my incentives so I made about $22,500. The Cowboy's called and said, "Drew, we want you to come in and we're going to give you a bonus for having such a great rookie year."

I said, "Oh, that's great. Cool!" I asked, "How much?"

They said, "We're going to give you $3,000."

I went to the Cowboy office and met with Gil Brandt. He made me sit out there for about half an hour because he did things like that. He finally let me in, put his arm around me, walked me down the hall, sat me down in a chair, and gave me a check.

He said, "You had a great rookie year. We appreciate the work ethic and the things you did, making the big plays, stepping up and starting." He gave me the check and it was for $2,500.

I said, "Gil, I thought you said I was getting $3,000."

He said, "Do you remember that $500 I gave you before you went to camp? We took that out of it."

What are you going to do, argue? I was still happy. I took the $2,500 and left.

CHAPTER NINETEEN
★★★★★

I had the job at Cullum and Boren after my rookie season and I needed it. Most of us were not making much money playing football and an off-season job was necessary just to keep the bills paid. When the NFL Players Association, headed by Ed Garvey and Gene Upshaw, talked strike in '74 just before training camp, I was concerned because we needed the money.

The Players Association theme was *No freedom, no football.* Our logo was a red, white and blue picture of a football player, fist raised in the air, symbolizing the strength and power that the players had. We didn't realize how much power we had as a group and it was tough convincing the constituency that a strike was the way to go.

Time was running out. I didn't worry about the salary because my salary wouldn't start until the season started. I needed the per diem money. That would have been enough to survive on.

The Players Association put pressure on us to hold out for the strike. The NFL put pressure on us, threatening that if we did hold out, we might lose our jobs. They threatened to bring in other players to replace us and it was a tough decision to make. Who should I go with? Do I go with the players or do I go with the league? I finally decided to side with the players. They had a strike fund and I had to hit that fund up a couple of times to get money to help deal with the possibility of a strike.

Eventually things got worked out. We went into training camp and there was no hold out. The threat was still hanging over our heads as players but the union orchestrated it all perfectly. We never walked out and we never had a work stoppage. It was significant at the time because it helped give the union some credibility. We didn't go on strike, but the threat of it sent a message to the NFL owners.

Going through that training camp was a little tough, because back home, my wife was pregnant and our baby was due any day. On July 23rd, after we had been in camp about a week, I got a call and went back to Dallas for the birth of our daughter, Tori Nicole.

The big edge was to go into training camp as a starter. There was going to be an issue with Otto Stowe if he was healthy. If they'd chosen Otto, I really couldn't have argued because Landry's philosophy was that you never lost your starting job because of an injury. If Otto had rehabilitated himself and coach told me he was the starter, I could have handled it. But he declared me as a starter because Otto was still rehabbing his ankle and was not ready. I went into that second season as a starter in training camp.

Before the 1974 season, Bob Hayes was traded to the 49ers. That's when Golden Richards stepped in as a starter. That was a tough situation because they brought Golden in to replace Bob and they forced it. Bob had some years left and could still play. He was effective because he was still the fastest guy on the team. As a matter of fact, he had a race with Golden. Golden's nickname was "White Lightning."

He was supposed to be The Great White Hope for Cowboys receivers. There were always people trying to instigate a race between Bob and Golden. But Bob wouldn't race him because he saw no need in it. However, they finally convinced Bob to race him. Bob said, "I'll do it, but only this way. I'll give him a one yard lead, and I'll beat him by a yard."

Guys were lined up on the sideline and bets were taken. For 40 yards guys lined up to see them race. Bob gave Golden that one-yard lead. Bob caught Golden and beat him by the same yard he had spotted him. We were all slapping five, saying "Bullet, Bullet. World's fastest human."

When I broke in, the Cowboys weren't using the shotgun. We implemented it in '74. I think we used it some in '73, but that was only if Roger wanted to. We didn't have all of the blocking set up. Coach Landry wanted to use the shotgun, but it was up to Roger to be comfortable with it and Roger was.

It was pretty much set that Roger was the starting quarterback, but Craig Morton was one good quarterback. Even our third string quarterback, Jack Concanon, had started a few years with the Chicago Bears. It was a battle between Roger and Craig because they were both capable of starting. It made both of them better. When you got down to it, Craig's pass was easier to catch. Craig's was pure, the classic release and the tight spiral.

We had a good season but it started off bad. We beat Atlanta the first game and then lost four straight. We got on a roll and won our next four. The tenth game of the season we played the Redskins at their place. We needed that game because we were 5-4 and if we lost, we were out of playoff contention.

It was a tough, physical game. They had the lead and we came back and had a chance to win it. Roger called me and I lined up on Mike Bass to run, a quick slant, five yards and in. Roger laid it in there and I went down to get it. He threw it low, which is what you want the quarterback to do in that situation, because if you don't get it, nobody else does. In an effort to make the catch, however, I lost sight of the ball. The next thing I knew, I dropped it. When the crowd started yelling, I knew that I had actually dropped that football. I was totally dejected. I can't say that the play cost us the game, but it could have won the game and kept our playoff hopes alive. I couldn't believe I dropped the ball in a critical situation. I couldn't believe I let the team and Roger down.

Two weeks later, on Thanksgiving Day, the Redskins came to Texas Stadium. I was fired up. It was payback time for me. That dropped ball in Washington had stayed in my mind constantly. I ran that same route in practice, over and over again, trying to simulate that situation in an effort to keep it from ever happening again.

The Cowboys and the Redskins hated each other. George Allen had come in, taken over and now the same Redskins that the Cowboys had beaten every year had been turned around. He'd made these same guys competitive and contenders. Now they were competing with us for the NFC East title on a yearly basis. The rivalry was heated. It was at a peak and starting to explode.

The Redskins were riding high because they were about to win the East and make the playoffs, and we were going to be out of the playoffs. We were mathematically eliminated after the game in Washington.

They came into Texas Stadium making a lot of noise. For this game, fuel was added to the fire when Diron Talbert, a defensive tackle, made a prediction. He said, "If we knock Staubach out of the game, we'll win the game."

They proceeded to knock Roger out of the game with a concussion. Clint Longley came in off the bench. We knew what Clint could do. We saw him every day in practice, and he had made great strides in his rookie year. To come from Abilene Christian College and become back-up quarterback with the Dallas Cowboys was a tremendous accomplishment. You don't achieve those kinds of accomplishments just because you're Clint Longley. You have to work and prove yourself. He did, all through training camp. He had a great training camp and we were impressed with him.

When Roger got knocked out in the third quarter, Clint came in with Washington ahead 16-3. We rallied around him and said, "Hey, you don't have to win it for us, just don't lose it". We got in the huddle and were surprised and shocked at this rookie's command. He took charge of the huddle, took charge of the game, called the plays – of course the plays came in from the sideline - and when he relayed those plays to the team in the huddle, he did it with authority like a seasoned veteran. Clint probably didn't even realize the pressure of the situation he faced. It was Thanksgiving Day, the game was on National TV, and he had just replaced Roger Staubach against the Washington Redskins. Like Blaine Nye said later, "It was a triumph of the uncluttered mind." Longley didn't realize where he was; he was just playing ball. It could have been at Abilene Christian, in the streets where he grew up or in high school. He was just playing football. He didn't care about all the things that were going on around him.

He hit Billy Joe for a touchdown. It put us within range of a comeback at 16-10. It was a perfect 35-yard pass to Billy Joe down the middle. Billy Joe caught it, stretched out, and went into the end zone untouched. We were excited and everyone was jumping all over the place, patting him on the back and congratulating him. We had some momentum. To tell the truth, I don't know if we would have had this momentum if Roger had stayed in the game. They pretty much had our number that day. They were shutting us down pretty well. When Roger got knocked out, it not only gave us the opportunity to rally around the young quarterback coming in, but it also pissed us off because they knocked out our leader. What really pissed us off was that they said they were going to do it, and they did.

When we got to the sideline we said, "We can win this game." Everyone was fired up. The defense held and we scored again but so did Washington. It got late in the fourth quarter and the Redskins led 23-17. We were down to a last chance drill. I lined up on the left side and saw Joe Theismann. I saw the arrogance in his face. I didn't hear what he was saying but I knew he was talking noise and rubbing it in. I saw George Allen. He was rubbing his hands, licking his thumb like he used to do. "Yeah, Pearson," I heard them saying, "We got ya this game. It's just a matter of time now. We told you we would knock Staubach out." They were yelling and I could hear it because I was flanked out on their side of the field.

We got to a do or die situation in the game with less than one minute left. In the huddle, I told Clint, "Let's run a turn in and take off on safety Kenny Stone".

He said, "Great, run it."

"O.K., call it."

He called it. Golden, who was on the other side, ran a post pattern. Billy Joe was lined up on my side and ran a crossing route. We were going to simulate that 16 route, which was becoming my bread and butter even though I was only in my second year. We ran that play often, especially in third-down situations. We got to the line of scrimmage, and the first thing I looked for was the defense. I saw the perfect defense. I could come off the line and if they were going to double me, there was only one way they could do it. That was with bracket coverage — one cornerback on the outside and a safty on the inside. The previous year we beat the same coverage in the playoff game when Roger hit me for that 83-yard touchdown. I knew I was going to fake the turn in, so all I cared about was Kenny Stone. I lined up wide to create space on the inside. When I came off the line, Clint was sure that it was the bracket coverage. Mike Bass had the outside and Stone's responsibility was to the inside. I came off the line with an outside release to widen Bass and get him out of the play and then weaved back in. Now I concentrated on Stone. I thought that Bass was too far away to make a play and he was. I took two steps in on Stone, and he thought it was going to be the 16 route which he probably studied all week in preparation for the game. He thought I was going to catch the ball over the middle and set us up in our territory to take some shots in the end zone in the final 30 seconds. I took those steps and he must have been hungry because he bit on the fake. I didn't even have to see him. I could feel him bite. I took it deep, looked back, and saw this rainbow pass coming down in a perfect spiral. Clint had already released it and I ran past both of those guys into the end zone.

It was a thrill to catch that pass. There was satisfaction in making that play in that situation to win the game after dropping the pass in RFK and losing the earlier game against them. Now I had my revenge, and even though we weren't in the playoffs, we still beat the Redskins. I was mobbed in the end zone by my teammates. I looked over at the sidelines and there was Theismann with his head down. There was Allen shaking his head; he couldn't believe what happened.

We kicked the extra point and won the game, 24-23.

Of course, from there, Clint Longley was the hero. I don't think he ever understood the magnitude of what he'd done. I can see him like it was yesterday. He didn't look like he was old enough to play in the NFL. He was smiling and grinning, holding the ball up. After the game we were interviewed on CBS to talk about the play.

In spite of the win, it was a disappointing year. Actually it was the only year in my eleven seasons with the Cowboys that we failed to make the playoffs. At least we finished the season strong with an 8-6 record after starting 1-4.

I had a great year with 1,087 yards receiving, and when the All-Pro honors came out, I made it. I couldn't believe it. I was an All-Pro wide receiver in the NFL, in only my second year, and I was feeling confident. I could play this game, create longevity, and have success.

CHAPTER TWENTY

★★★★★

Since we didn't make the playoffs in '74, our fans were thinking about rebuilding and expected that it was going to take a while for us to qualify for post season. We weren't thinking Super Bowl as we entered the '75 season. Coach Landry was realistic about the goals he set for our team. He always set an outstanding goal and a reasonable goal. If we didn't have the talent or the ability to win the Super Bowl, he wouldn't set that as a goal. The '75 season was the only time that winning the Super Bowl was not our outstanding goal. Our goal was to have a winning season and get back to the playoffs. Twelve rookies made the team in '75. Randy White and Thomas Henderson were the two No. 1 draft picks. Henderson was still Thomas at this point. He hadn't evolved into "Hollywood" yet. We had a good season. We turned it around and made the playoffs as a wild card team.

For the first playoff game, we went to Minnesota. We played the Vikings on December 28, 1975, in Bloomington. Most people didn't give us any chance to win. I don't know why we felt we could win, because the Vikings were loaded and heavily favored. They played us because they were the best team in the NFC, seeded No. 1, and we were the last seed. The best played the worst. We played in Metropolitan Stadium and it was the kind of atmosphere that I had only seen on TV as a kid. It was distinctive because it was a baseball stadium turned into a football field. It was part grass, part dirt, and both teams were on the same sideline.

I thought that Bud Grant, the Vikings coach, had specifically ordered this kind of day. It was 27 degrees, overcast, and cloudy. We came out trying to figure out whether we should wear gloves or not, long socks and long cleats, undershirt, or long sleeved shirt. The Vikings came out for pre-game warm-ups with short sleeve shirts, no gloves, no earmuffs, nothing. They tried to intimidate you. When you saw guys like Page, Marshall, Eller, Lurtsema and Yary come on the field, it *was* intimidating. We couldn't have heaters on our sideline because the Vikings didn't want heaters on theirs. One couldn't have it if the other didn't.

We had a bad start and didn't do anything offensively. We were shut out in the first half. I was upset most of the game because the ball wasn't coming to me. I didn't have a catch. The pattern was set that when we played the Vikings, Drew was not going to get many passes. We started playing better in the second half. We moved the ball against their great defense and scored in the third quarter. We came back in the fourth quarter with a field goal and were ahead, 10-7. This was a defensive battle — knock down, drag out, old-fashioned football. I had grown up watching many of the Vikings on TV, and now I was playing against them. It was my first playoff game on the road, and the situation was exciting.

We had the 10-7 lead but the Vikings started moving the ball in the fourth quarter. Brent McClanahan scored from the one at the end of an 11-play, 70-yard drive that took six minutes and ate up almost all of the quarter. We got the ball back and went three plays and out. They got the ball again. It was a blessing when our defense was able to stop them on three plays. They punted and we got the ball back on our 15 with 1:51 left. Fans were yelling, carrying on and thinking that they had the game won because this was the best Viking team that Bud Grant had assembled. There was no way we were going to go 85 yards against their defense in fewer than two minutes.

It didn't look good for us and I was upset because only one pass had been thrown to me all day. I couldn't believe we were losing. I thought that if they had thrown to me a little more, we wouldn't be in this situation. I was mad at Roger. I was mad at Landry. I was mad at everyone.

We were in a two-minute situation on our own 15. Roger and I really hadn't established ourselves as a combination. I had made some plays, but was not really the go-to guy. Golden and Billy Joe were in the huddle, but Roger asked me, "Drew, What you got?" I was upset, but now had a feeling of pride because I knew he was coming to me.

We were in the huddle and Roger said, "I'm coming to you on the sideline, Drew." We ran that first route for nine yards, which was easy because they were playing their version of a prevent defense. This would cost them later in the drive. Their prevent defense was the same defense they normally run; they just loosened up a little. We knew what they were going to do. A veteran team, they were not going to change. Minnesota believed in doing something, doing it well, and repeating it over and over. That's how they got to be so good.

We hit the first pass for nine and came back to the huddle. It was a harried situation. Roger threw an incomplete pass to Golden. He came back to me with another sideline route for seven yards. We were moving the ball pretty well. John Fitzgerald was snapping the ball and having trouble because he had an injured arm. We were also in the mud part of the field and he rolled one back to Roger. Roger ended up fumbling. He got sacked. Now we were second and 16. We came back with an incomplete pass and were third and 16. In the meantime, Kyle Davis, a rookie from OU who hadn't played much all season, came in and replaced Fitzgerald.

Davis came in and snapped it to Roger. It was his first play and it was an excellent snap. But now we faced a fourth down and 16. In the huddle Roger said, "Drew, What have you got? What can we do?"

I said, "Let's try a post corner on Nate Wright."

He said, "Yeah, that sounds good. "

We ran the post corner and the last thing Roger said when we broke the huddle was "Make sure you get enough for the first down." Sixteen yards. The odds of hitting this play were low, especially against the Vikings. So I lined up to the right on Nate Wright. This whole drive I was on Wright's side. It was designed that way because Wright played true man-to-man. He didn't sit back and read the quarterback like the other cornerback, Bobby Bryant. Plus, Roger was a little leery of Bryant, having thrown an interception in that playoff game in '73 against Bryant. Bryant was a smart player and when it looked like you had him beat, all of a sudden he'd read the quarterback, break on the ball, intercept or knock the ball down. Everything was designed for me to line up on the right side with Wright on the short hash mark.

I read their line-up and I knew it was going to be that 31-safety zone where the three guys just drop back, and if the receiver came in their area then they picked you up man-to-man. I knew they would drop back because Billy Joe was going to run the crossing route, and pull linebackers and the safety over. When I came into Wright's area, I knew I was going to be man-to-man. As I came off the line, the thing I wanted to do was use speed to close that gap between Nate and me as quickly as possible. I wanted to get up on his toes to make him think I was going to the post or was at least going deep. When I got up on his toes I gave him a shake and took it to the post. I faked it in more than normal. Usually on a post corner route, you might take it inside two, at the most, three steps. I took this about four or five steps and I felt him on me. When I felt that pressure I broke it back out to the sideline.

The key was that when I broke to the sideline, I didn't break at an angle, I flattened it off. Roger and I connected on this play a million times in practice. It wasn't an accident that he read me flattening it off like that. We had worked on this a long time. I looked back, the ball was coming, and Roger made a perfect pass. Wright recovered and if he hadn't hit me I would have been able to get my feet in bounds, but he hit me and knocked me out of bounds. The ref called it a force out, good catch, 22 yards and a first down. They told me later that after I caught the ball, I was sliding along a snow bank and a security guard kicked me. I didn't feel it then, because my adrenaline was flowing. When you catch a fourth and 16 for 22 yards, you don't worry about a security guard kicking you.

We were now on the 50-yard line. Back to the huddle, Roger said, "Drew, What have you got?" I had no breath. I was really sucking air. He said, "O.K., I'll run a play to the other side." He called a swing pass to Preston Pearson. As it turned out, that play could have cost us because Preston was wide open but dropped it with 37 seconds left. I like to say that Preston, being a smart teammate and a Pearson, dropped the pass on purpose. He knew if he caught the ball, we'd be in the middle of the field with no time outs, and only thirty-some seconds left. The Vikings would tackle him, hold him down, and maybe we would get to line up for one more play. By dropping the ball, Preston stopped the clock. We were able to huddle and call a play. Roger said, "Drew, remember when you ran the turn and take-off last year against Washington to beat the Redskins?"

I said, "Yeah." But I was thinking, *Do you remember it? You were knocked out that game.*

He said, "Run it," then he said to Golden Richards, "Run a good post pattern." We weren't so concerned about Wright, because we knew they were going to play that same defense and he was going to be on me man-to-man. Our concern was Paul Krause, the safety. He played a deep center field. So, if you were going deep, you didn't want him coming over trying to help Nate. Roger told Golden, " I'm going to pump the post to get Krause to go to that side of the field."

We got to the line of scrimmage and Roger took the snap. Golden ran a great post pattern, a believable post pattern, and Krause followed Golden because Roger's eyes took him there. When Roger pumped, Krause jumped the route and left me man-to-man on Wright. I used the same philosophy as the post corner on fourth and 16. I wanted to close the gap between Nate and me. I wanted him to feel the pressure of what I might do. I wanted him to wonder, *Is he going in, going to post, going to the corner, or is he going straight up?* I put him in that bind and he bit on the play. I felt him lean and then I took it deep. My biggest concern going deep was to avoid colliding with him. I avoided him and as we ran down the field, he was right with me.

I figured I had a 50/50 chance in this situation. At first I thought Roger was going to throw that ball away. I thought I had one more gear I could use to separate from Nate and make the catch. I would catch it going away in the end zone, spike it, and that would be the game. By pumping so deliberately Roger took Krause out of the play. By the time Roger threw the ball, I had run my route and I was far down field.

I looked back while running neck and neck with Nate. I saw that the ball was under thrown. Nate was looking at me, gauging my reaction. When I looked back he was going to turn to try to look back himself. With him doing that, I was able to use what we receivers refer to as the swim move. We usually use it coming off the line to gain position on a defensive back. You engage him in his shoulder or his elbow with your left hand. With your right hand, you come over the top, which gives you inside position. So that's what I used. There was contact on the play, like two players jostling for position. When I brought my right arm over, there was contact with Wright. There was no deliberate push. I've been asked this question many times. Cowboy fans believe me; Viking fans don't. With that contact, Nate fell down and when I brought my arm around, the ball was there. It hit my hands and I thought, *Oh man, I got it*. Then it went right through my hands. I thought, *Oh, no!* But I was bent over and being bent over, I was able to stop the momentum of the ball enough with my hands that it stuck between my elbow and my hip. I actually caught the football with my elbow and my hip. I looked down and thought, *I caught it. Let me get in the end zone.*

After I caught the ball, I looked to see if there were any flags. The first thing I saw was an orange object. I said, "Oh no, they've called pass interference." I was sure something was going to be called, either defensive or offensive pass interference. I saw this orange thing, and then I watched it hit the ground and keep rolling. Well, I'd never seen a flag hit the ground and roll so I knew it wasn't a penalty. It was an orange. I backed into the end zone untouched. Krause came across the field complaining to the ref. The next thing I knew, a whisky bottle sailed out of the stands and hit one of the referees in the head. It knocked him cold.

The night before a game, I always tried to picture myself in key situations. So when I made a play like that, it was almost de ja vu. I pictured myself making the winning catch. I did this before every game, and for some reason, I had it in my mind that if I caught a touchdown in this playoff game, I was going to throw the football in the stands. After I caught the Hail Mary, I was in the back of the end zone, and the first one to greet me was Golden Richards. He hugged me until I pulled away from him with the football. I turned toward the stands in the end zone and threw the ball as far as I could. I threw it over the scoreboard and into the parking lot.

I had this premonition that I was going to throw the ball into the stands. That's O.K. if you're playing at home but if you do it on the road, you're giving the other team a souvenir. I wish I had kept the football, but I lived up to my vision and threw it away. To this day, no one has approached me to say, "This is the Hail Mary ball." I've signed everything — tickets from the game, programs from the game, and I've talked to people who were there, but nobody has come up with the football. It's something I wish I had now.

To get back to our bench, we had to walk past the Vikings bench and as I trotted back, I could feel their pain and frustration. The official who was hit in the head with the bottle was replaced, and then we kicked off. We shut them down on three plays with Tarkenton getting sacked on two of them. After we won 17-14, the stadium was stunned. Rayfield Wright and Jethro Pugh, two of our biggest guys, said, "Drew, you get between us." They escorted me off the field because I needed protection to get in the locker room. As we got close to the end zone tunnel leading to our locker room, someone yelled out, "Drew!" Naturally, I reacted. The next thing I knew, here came a cup of beer right in my face. Rayfield was going to go get the guy, but I said, "No, no, let him go." We ended up rushing into the locker room and it was mayhem. People were congratulating, pumping, slapping, and everybody was beating on me. A mass of reporters were there.

At first the reporters were all around Roger's locker. They asked Roger about the play and one of them mentioned that I ran into the end zone. "You mean Drew caught the ball and ran in for the touchdown?" replied Roger, who was hit as soon as he released the ball. "I just threw the ball as far as I could and said a 'Hail Mary'."

The media picked up on it and **Hail Mary** became a part of sports vernacular. Any last minute situation, whether it's catching a touchdown pass, running a touchdown in to win the game, hitting a home run in the bottom of the ninth, or getting the final shot at the buzzer, is now referred to as Hail Mary. The play is now part of every team's playbook — Hail Mary right, Hail Mary left or Hail Mary down the middle. I know Roger didn't plan that. Roger is Catholic, and that's what came to his mind. When he threw the football he said a Hail Mary and I answered his prayer by making the catch.

It was great celebrating in the locker room. Everyone was excited. We did, however, get some bad news. Word was circulating through the locker room that Fran Tarkenton's father had passed away from a heart attack. They said he was sitting, watching the game, and right after that play he had a heart attack and died. That news changed the atmosphere to a more somber tone. Football players are brothers in this fraternity. We all care about each other because we know what it takes to play this game. Hearing something like that was a shock.

We loaded the bus and got out of there to catch our flight back home. Despite the news about Fran's dad, we were still excited. I don't think anybody sat down between take off and landing. The flight attendants were like "Forget it." There was no sense making any announcements. It was just party time. Coach Landry used to let us have two beers. That was our limit, so we had a two-beer celebration.

When we touched down in Dallas the pilot came on and said, "There are a ton of people out here at the airport. We don't know what we're going to do." He thought about going to another hanger to let us off because the crowd was causing a big jam in the airport. This was DFW when it was fairly new and many people hadn't been out there and didn't know how to maneuver.

We decided to go to the gate. When the Braniff plane pulled into the gate, all of the guys said, "Drew, you go up there. You get off first. " They figured if I got off, the crowd would follow me and they could sneak through. I couldn't believe it when I walked off that plane. I'd never experienced anything like it in my life. A throng of people, all Cowboys fans, were hanging over the partitions and standing on chairs. Dads had kids on their shoulders. It was bedlam. One of the first persons I saw was Marsha. She ran up and hugged me. Everyone was pounding on me and the TV cameras had their lights shining. They tried to do interviews. It was wild. I don't think that you could do anything like that today for security reasons. Back then we didn't have those concerns.

When I got home my phone rang constantly. Friends, relatives, my Mom, my Dad, everyone called. They said, "I saw the game, but tell me about it anyway." I described the play at least 50 times. It was exciting, awesome. I could have run for mayor or asked for anything that day, or even that week, and every request would have been honored. I was the man. I'd had three consecutive seasons of making a clutch catch to win a game. They now called me, "Mr. Clutch."

CHAPTER TWENTY-ONE
★★★★★

We went to L.A. the next week to play the Rams for the NFC Championship and completely dismantled them. They were the favorite and we were still only the wild card team. Our defense was on, the offense was on, and we had a great game plan. Coach Landry brought us back to earth quickly after the Minnesota game. In our meeting at 2:00 p.m. on Monday he told us it was great but we hadn't accomplished our goal. He had just reclassified our goal. Now our outstanding goal was to win the Super Bowl. We earned that right. Our reasonable goal had been to make the playoffs. We had gone to Bloomington and won our first playoff game, so now our outstanding goal was to go all the way.

The weather was different from what we had experienced the week before in Minnesota. That's what pro football is all about. That's part of the reason they call it professional football. As a player, you have to be professional and make adjustments. We never discussed the weather or the conditions we were going to play in. We considered it in regard to the equipment we wore, or what kind of surfaces we were playing on. The weather was something that was accepted because you were a professional. So we went from 27 degrees one week to 75 degrees the next week and we were supposed to make that adjustment. If you had to adjust, it's better to go from 27 to 75 degrees than from 75 to 27. That's for sure.

We beat the Rams 37-7 in front of 84,000 people to qualify for Super Bowl X. We were ecstatic. It was supposed to be a rebuilding year, we had 12 rookies, and the Cowboys were back in the Super Bowl anyway. It was a big deal — my first Super Bowl and against the Pittsburgh Steelers. We felt that the Steelers might have better talent, but we were the team of destiny. We had great coaching, great players, and felt we had a solid chance to win the game.

I received calls from many relatives. The more success we had, the more relatives called. Success is relative. Relatives were coming out of the woodwork. Everyone wanted Super Bowl tickets.

I had a disappointment early in the week while we were preparing for the big game. After I caught the Hail Mary, *Sports Illustrated* came out with the game as their lead story and mistakenly put Preston Pearson's picture on the cover. I asked *Sports Illustrated* why they picked Preston when I caught the Hail Mary. An editor from *Sports Illustrated* sent me a letter apologizing because they made the mistake. They were supposed to put me on the cover, but because of the same last name, Preston Pearson was on the cover. This was my one opportunity, maybe my one chance in my life to be on the cover of *Sports Illustrated*, and they put Preston there instead of me. They sent me a framed picture of the Hail Mary catch. I thought, *This is nice. I appreciate it but it's not the same.* As it turned out, that was my only opportunity to make the cover of *Sports Illustrated*. It was one of the many ironies that marked my career.

I was also disappointed that week because we got word that eight Cowboys had been selected to participate in the Super Teams competition in Hawaii. Golden Richards was chosen over me. Coach Landry recognized the snub and mentioned something to me about it. He said. "Don't worry about it. It's one of those things. You know your value to the team." All of the players consoled me because they felt and understood my disappointment. I got past that because we had to concentrate on the game, and that was the most important thing.

Going to a Super Bowl for the first time, I wasn't aware that there were so many distractions. You think that you are It. Amazing how everybody wants a piece of you. It was that way for everyone on the team. If you were associated with the Cowboys, everybody wanted a piece.

Because Coach Landry and most of the staff had experienced Super Bowls, he knew how to deal with it. He told us, "Make sure you take care of all of your business early. Get your tickets, your rooms, and find out who is coming." He gave us a couple of days off after the Championship Game to do that. We didn't practice until the Wednesday of the dead week before the Super Bowl. You thought you had it all under control, but your phone rang continuously with people trying to get to the game and get tickets.

We had a good week of practice and a good game plan for the Steelers. We knew that they were an extremely physical team. As receivers, we had to deal with the coverage of Mel Blount and Ron Johnson. They were physical cornerbacks. They would not let you go inside on any pass route on third down. Coach Landry tried to find a way that we could maneuver inside because that was the only way wide receivers would be effective working against their pass defense. If you took outside releases every time, they came up and bumped you. That was what they wanted because then you could only work part of the field. If you could get inside, you would put them in a bind because they wouldn't know whether you were going in or out on your pass route.

All week long Coach Landry said, "We've got to get inside against the Steelers." We worked on a maneuver that he designed. When he first demonstrated, it was funny because Coach Landry limped when he ran from knee injuries he suffered when he played for the New York Giants. He tried to simulate a receiver running a pass route against the Pittsburgh defense and hip-hopped through the pattern.

I thought, *Coach, if I run it like that, we'll never get inside.* He demonstrated it all week long — three steps to the outside, get them going up field, and break underneath. That's what we practiced all week. Golden and I said, "Yeah, we can do this. We can be physical." We even pumped a little iron that week because we knew we had to get inside. We worked on our hand techniques to maneuver into position. After the third day of practicing, even our guys weren't letting us inside. Our lack of success in practice lead me to think, *If I'm going to catch any passes in this Super Bowl, it's going to come on first or second down because they're really going to take away the outside.*

We boarded a plane, flew to Miami and what a thrill that was! We landed and got off the plane as NFC champions. The media was there and fans were all over the place. It was just what I'd been told the Super Bowl was all about. It was a spectacle. We rode the bus up to Ft. Lauderdale.

All of my immediate family, including brothers and sisters,

were there. My cousin, his friend, my Dad and his buddies were there. We stayed at the Galt Ocean Mile. I couldn't believe we were staying in this hotel as we prepared for the Super Bowl. It was not one of the nicest hotels I've ever been in.

My Dad was in heaven. You'd think he caught the Hail Mary because he was telling the stories. I'm more of a low key guy, but my parents were so excited about their son playing for the Cowboys that they weren't low key about anything. They would tell people, "I'm Drew Pearson's father," or "I'm Drew Pearson's mother." My Dad held court in the lobby. I'd go down there and he had tons of people around him. He signed autographs and had the time of his life. That's the kind of thing that playing in those games does. It doesn't just benefit you; it benefits your family and everyone connected to you.

We had a great week of practice. Waiting two weeks for the game to start had been agonizing, because we were ready to play. First of all, we had momentum from the Hail Mary game in Minnesota and the Championship Game in L.A. and we didn't want to take a week off. But, at the same time, we knew that delay was part of the process.

We were anxious for the game to start. But there was one good thing about that week of practice in Miami. Every time we went to the locker room there were different gifts in our stalls. Adidas was the big clothing manufacturer then, and there were Adidas sweats and Adidas shoes. There were also items from Puma and Pony, which were just getting started back then. Every time we got off the bus, there was suspense to see what had been left in our lockers. Because we weren't making much money, free stuff meant a lot. We wanted to look like athletes; like we had some of the better stuff because we were professionals.

It was a relief to get to the Orange Bowl game site. We put

on uniforms and equipment in individual ways. My ritual was related to the way I dressed. Everything had to be put on the right side first. I put the right sock on before the left sock, the right shoe before the left, the right leg into the pants before the left, and the right arm into the sleeve before the left. Sometimes I did it subconsciously and remembered that I'd done it wrong. Then I'd go back and do it again. I didn't want anything to jinx me because it was a big game and my first Super Bowl.

After we got dressed, the locker room was quiet. I guess this was how you prepared for a Super Bowl. We had a lot of veterans and they knew how to handle themselves in this situation. As first timers, we watched and emulated them. We went out on the field to test the Orange Bowl surface. It was a good thing that we did because it was one sorry, worn out turf. I couldn't believe we were playing the Super Bowl on this turf.

My objective for pre-game was to get loose and ready for the game. When you're a wide receiver, you have to be stylish. I used to do a drill where I caught the ball with one hand. I knew the fans watched and I knew they said, "I can't believe he's doing that kind of stuff." It was a little show for me.

We had a good team but we knew we had to play a perfect game to beat the Steelers. With all of the games I had played to that point, nothing compared to the first Super Bowl. The spectacle, the importance, and the excitement were magnified. The player intro's, going to the game and, having our busses escorted to the Orange Bowl, watching the Cowboy and Steeler fans tailgate added to the pre-game drama. Even the adrenaline flowing in the locker room as we dressed and got psyched to play was at a higher level than any game that I had experienced. It was a pressure-packed situation, but one I relished. This was what we had worked for. To be introduced and run on that field knowing that I had come in as a free agent at $14,500, and now started for the Dallas Cowboys in the Super Bowl was a tremendous high. It was something I'll never forget and that I'll always cherish and appreciate.

Pittsburgh kicked off to begin the game, and early on we moved the ball. Roger called one of our favorite plays. I lined up to the right in on what we called the short divide. I went in motion and Roger snapped the ball before I reached Billy Joe, the tight end. Billy Joe ran a five-yard route underneath to keep the linebackers up. I ran a deep spurt route. On the other side, Golden ran a post pattern to clear things out as we came across. Roger's job was to read the linebackers. If the linebackers dropped back, he dumped a pass to Billy Joe. If they were up, he hit me. The linebackers were up. I came across, Roger hit me and I took it in for a 34-yard touchdown. I remember scoring a Super Bowl touchdown and thinking, *Now this is really getting good.*

That gave us confidence but it also woke up Pittsburgh. The Steelers knew they had a battle on their hands. We made some plays, but Lynn Swann had a phenomenal game. He had the game that you dream about in the Super Bowl. He made spectacular catches, one of them a 64-yard touchdown. We had Franco Harris shut down and Terry Bradshaw under control, but Swann was the difference for them offensively. Their defense was also strong. We ended up losing that Super Bowl, 21-17.

I was disappointed and hurt. We had a chance to get a Super Bowl ring. As any athlete going for a title knows, when you get that close and lose, you wonder if you'll get that close again. There was disappointment in our locker room. Many players cried. Coach Landry tried to console and comfort us. He said that we'd had a great season because no one expected us to go to the Super Bowl. He said he hoped it would inspire us in the off-season to come back next year and win it.

The next year, 1976, we came back 11-3. In a ten-game stretch, we won nine. Then we suffered a disappointment when we lost to the Rams in Dallas in the divisional playoffs. The score was 14-12. Our offense never got anything going. The defense played well enough to win, but after scoring almost 300 points in the regular season, we couldn't get 15 in the playoff game against the Rams.

CHAPTER TWENTY-TWO
★★★★★

The 1975 Super Bowl was a tremendous thrill, and fortunately for me, I was able to play in two more Super Bowls. The most memorable, of course was in '77 when we played the Denver Broncos in New Orleans. Again, the atmosphere and excitement were outrageous. This was Denver's first Super Bowl and they had overcome tremendous odds to turn their team around. Red Miller was their coach and he was "Mr. Everything" in Denver. They had the Orange Crush theme going: "We're going to orange crush the Cowboys." We had played them in the final regular season game and had beaten them, but they were physical. I remember Billy Thompson decking me on a crossing route. I still feel that collision in some places.

We knew that we were the better team and we played a great game. Coach Landry's preparation was unbelievable, especially in big games. We knew all of Denver's tendencies. We also had confidence because Craig Morton was their quarterback. We knew how to play Craig and Coach Landry knew how to defense him. When Craig went back to pass, you had to blitz everyone. We had to let him know that we were coming after him because he was not a mobile quarterback. He was a pocket passer. He didn't even try to run. If you could collapse the pocket around him, you had him. Eventually, we knocked him out of the game.

We executed well on offense. Butch Johnson made a nice catch in the end zone on a post pattern from Roger. I was pretty much a decoy the whole game. I knew this going in because I'd seen the game plan. I knew what my role was going to be. If I caught any passes it was going to be on first or second down.

I had a chance to catch a touchdown on the slant route. If I dropped a pass it was always on that route. I think I had a tendency to take my eye off the ball. Again, it was a perfect pass, low and away, and when I went down to get it, it went off my arm. I looked up and I could not believe that I'd dropped a pass in the Super Bowl. I blamed it on my shoes. My thing was to tape my shoes to my feet. I taped my ankles, wore two pair of socks, and taped my shoes to my feet. Before this game, I worked out a deal with Adidas. They were going to give me apparel in return for wearing their shoes. I said, "I'll wear your shoes, but I've got to tape them on."

They said, "If you tape them you'll cover the stripes." So, they came up with this idea of putting decals on my shoes. After I taped my shoes, I put three stripes on the side of the shoe to show the Adidas logo. I was in good standing with them, but it looked ugly. I was the type player who had to look right to play right, and my feet looked ugly. I think to this day that's the reason I dropped that ball in the end zone.

We broke the game open. Coach Landry came up with a fullback pass from Robert Newhouse. Nobody thought that Newhouse could throw a pass, especially going to his left. The play began like a fullback sweep. Roger pitched the ball to Newhouse and he took it to the left like he was running a sweep, then stopped and turned. Golden did a stutter route like he was going to block the cornerback. When he felt that cornerback come up, he released and went behind him. Newhouse laid out a perfect pass and Golden made a great catch over his shoulder in the end zone for a touchdown. That blew the game wide open. We were slapping five on the sidelines, talking about the money we'd won.

Defense had an awesome game and forced eight turnovers. Four or five different guys on defense could have been selected as Most Valuable Player of the game. Harvey Martin and Randy White were co-MVP's, but Too Tall Jones could have gotten it and Randy Hughes had a phenomenal game.

My friends and family were at the party afterwards. It was the culmination of a great season. We had lost only three regular season games. Offense averaged close to 30 points and defense shut people down. If you could get more than 13 points on our defense, you were doing something.

We had a phenomenal football team. It was Tony Dorsett's rookie year and he added another dimension to our offense. It was amazing that with all of his accomplishments, Landry did not start him immediately. Dorsett didn't start until midway through the season. That was really tough for Tony to take, coming off winning the Heisman Trophy and a national college championship. He was used to being the man who carried the ball 35-40 times a game. Tony complained about it, but he eventually understood what Coach Landry was trying to do. Preston started for most of the season but when Coach Landry felt Tony was ready, he put him in there.

In Tony's second year, 1978, there was no question that he was going to be the starter. He had rare ability. Our first game in '78 was against Baltimore. They were the Colts then. We played on Monday Night Football, and it rained like crazy. I remember one play where Dorsett burst for 80 yards. He got to about the 20-yard line and there was nobody there but Tony Hill and me, escorting Dorsett into the end zone. We were slapping five on the 20-yard line. I held hands with Tony Hill while Dorsett trotted into the end zone.

Dorsett brought a new dimension to our offense. He wasn't just a great running back. He was a breakaway running back. We were a high-powered offense. Even though we were conservative, we had many explosive players who could get deep and make big plays. When we added Dorsett, it just made us even more effective.

Defense also got better and we returned to the Super Bowl in 1978. We breezed through the playoffs. We played the Steelers again and thought, *Hey, we're better than them this time around.* We knew that the tables were turned and that we should beat these guys.

We had another great game plan. Coach Landry called a lot of deceptives. We never called them trick plays or flea flickers. We called them deceptives. Coach Landry actually opened the first series with a deceptive. Roger took the snap, and pitched to Dorsett. I came around on the reverse and took the hand off from him. I then threw a pass to Billy Joe.

We ran the play to perfection in practice. I was excited to get a chance to throw a touchdown in the Super Bowl. I was pumped up — maybe a little too pumped. When I came across the backfield, Mel Blount trailed me. When I got to the end, he shot up to the line of scrimmage and I thought Mel was on my tail. I sped up the hand-off between Tony and me and in that movement, we fumbled and the Steelers recovered. The sad thing about losing the ball, was that Billy

Joe was uncovered. He came to the sideline and said, "Spike, I was wide open."

I said, "Damn, we would have had our touchdown in the Super Bowl."

We made too many mistakes. Randy White fumbled a kickoff return. He was in the wedge, and they kicked it short. He caught the ball with a cast on his arm and instead of pitching it to the running back, he tried to run with it. They hit him, the ball went flying and they recovered. It gave Pittsburgh momentum to get another score. Jackie Smith also dropped a pass in the end zone. We moved the ball, but another problem was that we opened up our offense too late.

Coach Landry was a little too conservative. When our defense was sharp, the offense got conservative. When our defense struggled we opened up our offense to compete with them and keep up with the scoring. Our defense played a good game, but the Steelers were loaded with great athletes. Swann and Stallworth made big plays and Rocky Bleier caught a touchdown. They also had Franco Harris and Bradshaw. Roger kept asking me, "What have you got, Drew?"

I was working against Mel Blount, Donnie Shell, Mike Wagner and Ron Johnson. Johnson never got much publicity. He got lost in the shuffle of great teammates, but he was a physical player. With the type defense they played, you didn't run free like you did against Minnesota. When you came off the line, you got bumped and hit.

I remember one third down play before Butch Johnson scored the touchdown to make it 35-31. Roger drilled the pass. I sprinted to reach a high pass — a blessing because that's where the ball needed to be to make the play. I jumped to get it. I ended up catching the ball by trapping it between my pads and hands. As soon as I did Wagner nailed me in the ribs. I went limp. Then the rest of the Steelers came, bam,

bam, bam and drove me to the ground. Preston tried to knock some people off. I caught the ball for a first down, but ended up cracking two ribs. I felt like I couldn't breathe. Butch Johnson replaced me. He caught a four-yard touchdown pass that should have been mine on the next play.

We were devastated that we'd lost. My ribs were killing me. Even though we lost, the Cowboys set up a party for family and friends after the game. I couldn't go. I had to take codeine to deal with the pain. All I did after that game was lie in bed. I couldn't move, I couldn't laugh, I couldn't do anything. The pain was compounded by the loss. We felt that we should have won that game. The best thing about Super Bowl XIII was that people still claim that it was one of the most exciting Super Bowls ever played. It was certainly one of the highest scoring games.

It would have been nice to win back-to-back Super Bowls. It would have been nice to beat the Steelers in a situation where it counted. During my whole career, I never beat the Steelers in a meaningful game. The only time I ever beat them was in an exhibition game. We lost regular season games and Super Bowl games against them. If one team had our number, it was the Pittsburgh Steelers.

CHAPTER TWENTY-THREE
★★★★★

Jethro Pugh and "Too Tall" Jones retired before the **1979** season and Charlie Waters was lost to injury during preseason. After starting 8-2, we lost three straight games and Coach Landry cut Thomas Henderson. This was a wake up call to the team and the next two games resulted in victories. The last game of the regular season was at Texas Stadium against the Redskins. No one knew at the time, but it would be Roger Staubach's final regular season game.

The game was a roller coaster ride. Washington jumped ahead 17-0 only to see us come back to take a 21-17 lead. Washington proceeded to score the next 17 points and led, 34-21. With four minutes left Washington fumbled and one last Staubach miracle was underway. Staubach hit Ron Springs with a 26-yard touchdown pass to close the gap to 34-28. The defense held and the Redskins were forced to punt with 1:46 left in the game. With 45 seconds left, Staubach hit Tony Hill with a seven-yard touchdown and we had a 35-34 season-ending win.

We played the Rams in Texas Stadium the first game of the

playoffs and trailed 14-5 at half. We scored two touchdowns to take a 19-14 lead and it looked like another come-from-behind win but the defense couldn't hold the lead and we lost 21-19 on a 50 yard touchdown pass late in the Fourth quarter.

Staubach was outstanding in his final season, he threw 27 touchdown passes and only 11 interceptions. I had a good year, catching 55 passes good for 1,026 yards and eight touchdowns.

The **1980** season was my first without Roger. Danny White proved that he was a better athlete and leader than many thought. The season was an up-and-down experience. We started 5-1, and then went 2-2. We won five of the final six and were a wild card entry to the playoffs.

Offensively, we scored the second most points (454) in the NFC but our defense was shaky. Tony Hill became the go to guy and I had only 568 yards and six scores on 43 receptions.

One of the most devastating things I dealt with during my playing time with the Cowboys was my father's illness. It was a tough time because my father had never been sick, at least not that we knew about.

Dad never went to the doctor. Apparently, he'd had a problem with his lungs for a long time. He didn't get it treated until a tumor developed that was so big it protruded from his chest. He hid it from us and we didn't even know there was a problem, or that the tumor was there.

He received nothing but the best as far as treatment. However, the tumor was so huge, doctors couldn't do surgery. At the same time, the doctors gave us hope that they could do something about it. We admitted Dad to the Sloan Kettering Hospital in New York, the most renowned cancer treatment facility in the United States.

I drove a van to New Jersey, to help him get back and forth to New York for treatments. I flew there several times to see him in the hospital and it was a frustrating experience. I was disappointed that I couldn't do more to help him. To see my dad going through that and being so weak was difficult. He'd be in good spirits before his treatments. Then the chemo and radiation zapped him to the point that he could hardly walk. My dad was outgoing, happy-go-lucky, always the life of the party. To see him down and hurting was depressing.

He was tough but it got to a point where he wasn't going to make it. When he realized that, he was devastated. He was 53 years old, my present age. Considering the size of the tumor and its location, it was amazing he lasted that long.

We played the Giants in Giants Stadium on November 9 and lost the game. It was the first time the Giants beat us there in a while. We were disappointed in the loss. I asked Coach Landry if I could stay over and come back on Monday morning. I wanted to go visit Dad at his house. Coach Landry agreed with no hesitation.

I disappointed my father on this visit. I sat with him all day and that night after the game. He was upset that we had lost. After everyone went to work on Monday, I sat with him most of the day. I only had one shirt with me because we traveled light. I told Dad "I'm going to run to the store real quick and buy a shirt.

He said, "Fine." He asked me to be back soon because his boss was coming to the house, and he wanted me to meet him. He was worried about his job.

I went to the store, lollygagged around and didn't realize that my watch was set on Dallas time. Jersey time was an hour later. When

I got to the house, I saw the sadness in my Dad's face. I asked him, "What's wrong?"

He said, "Damn, Drew. I told you all I wanted was for you to be here when my boss got here."

I asked, "Where is he? Is he coming?"

Dad said, "He's been here already. He's gone."

I felt so bad that I didn't want to leave. I said, "I'm sorry Dad." I offered to call his boss, but Dad was mad and didn't want to deal with it. That made it hard for me to leave, but I had to. As it turned out, this was the last time I saw him alive.

I knew going into the Redskins game on November 23, 1980, that Dad was in bad shape, because my sister called to tell me. He didn't want me to miss any games or practices so there was no doubt that I had to play. Of course, everything I did at that point was for my Dad. Playing and getting hit didn't mean anything compared to what he was going through.

At halftime I looked in the stands to find Marsha so she could acknowledge that everything was all right. When I looked for her, she wasn't there and I knew something was wrong. Normally, I was the last one into the tunnel, out of the locker room, off the field. I never liked to walk in the crowd. I liked to walk separate. The team went up the tunnel and I trailed behind. I saw Coach Landry standing up at the top of the tunnel. When I looked up and saw him, his image never looked bigger. Once we were inside the tunnel, there was a media room where we did our interviews after the game. Coach Landry told me to come in there. Marsha was there and she was crying. He didn't have to tell me. I said, "No, no, no! Don't tell me, don't tell me." My father passed away during the first half of the game. I bawled like a baby, Marsha was crying, and Coach Landry had tears in his eyes.

We were in a big game, a close game. This was the Redskins. We won it 14-10. Instead of going to the locker room to deal with the X's and O's of the second half, Coach Laundry stayed in the media room consoling me. The last thing he said was, "It is up to you. You don't have to play this half. You can leave now and take care of your business and that will be fine. There'll be no questions asked. I'll let everybody know why you left."

I sat there with my head in my hands, rubbing my eyes and said, "Coach, you know what? I can't leave. My Dad wouldn't want me to leave. I've got to play the second half." I played the second half and no one in the stands knew. My teammates knew because Coach Landry and I had been conspicuous in our absence from the locker room. Harvey, "Too Tall", and Billy Joe knew that my Dad was sick. They were fans of my Dad. On away games, he would be there pumping them and talking to them like they were his sons.

Harvey came to me when we went back on the field and said, "Homeboy, I'm sorry and we're gonna kick some Redskin butt for your Dad." They played that half for my Dad and we ended up winning the game.

We played Seattle on Thanksgiving Day so they purposely planned Dad's funeral on Friday. No one expected me to come back for the Thursday game. I left for Jersey after the game on Sunday, and didn't have any contact with anyone from the Cowboys organization until I came back. I returned that Wednesday before the Thursday game. The plane was late. I tried to get back in time to practice. I wanted to play; I needed to play. I didn't make it back on time because the plane was delayed. When I got to the practice field, the team was getting ready to start practice. I went in and put my uniform on, taped my ankles and came out of the locker room. Everyone on the team turned to see who was coming out of the locker room. When they saw that No. 88 on the practice jersey, they were shocked.

I took two laps around the field, which we did before every practice and then went to the huddle. Nobody said anything. Nobody knew what to say. When we got into the locker room, Coach Landry called me in and said, "We were surprised to see you. We didn't expect you back." He talked about the situation with my Dad and told me he was sorry for my loss. Then he said, "I'm going to let Butch Johnson start." I didn't argue, but I was hurt. I wanted to play; I needed to play.

I wasn't in the frame of mind to argue or protest what Coach Landry said so I just said, "O.K." Butch started and by this time everyone knew that my father had died. We played the game with me standing on the sideline. It was one of the hardest things I ever did, I stood, not being able to release any frustration. I was angry, disappointed and hurt.

Coach put me in the game in the second half. I had only one pass thrown to me and I caught it. We killed Seattle and I didn't even have to play. When I went in, Danny White called me on the 16 route. We didn't need it. We were way ahead and could have run the clock out. But, he called that old 16 route. Coach Landry had to have something to do with that, too, because he called the plays. I lined up to the left and I thought *I don't care if Danny throws this ball downtown; I'm going to get it.* As soon as I caught it, I got hit and lay on the ground then I held the ball up to let the fans know I had the ball and the first down.

The fans went wild! It may have been a meaningless pass in a game that was already over but the fans knew what that was all about. They knew my father had passed away. They knew that I had been gone, come back to play the game, and made the catch in Drew Pearson style. I said to myself, *That was my Dad making that play for me.*

I dedicated every game and every play for the rest of the

season to my Dad. We made the playoffs. We beat the Rams in the first round of the playoffs. Then we played Atlanta in the divisional playoff game. Atlanta was hot because it was the Falcons' first time to make the playoffs for a while, and the Georgia Bulldogs, led by Herschel Walker, had won the national collegiate championship. Their stadium was packed and it was a great atmosphere. It was a late game so by the time we kicked off it was dark. The lights were on, and it was a good atmosphere for a playoff game.

I remember the last thing Coach Landry said before we left that locker room. He said, " We're going to run into a buzz-saw out there. What we've got to do is see where we are when the dust settles and that dust will usually settle after the first quarter." When the dust settled, we were down 14-0. They were whipping our butts up and down the field. We couldn't do anything offensively. They were scoring at will. They hit two long passes to set up touchdowns and hit a long one to score.

In the second half, we were down two touchdowns with 4: 28 left on a hot and humid night. I was cramping up, big time. We were behind all game, so we kept passing. I did a lot of running. I got sick to my stomach before every game I played in the NFL, and often when I went to the sideline I threw up. Coming to the sideline, instead of handing me a bottle of Gatorade or water, the doctor handed me a bottle of Mylanta or Maalox. I drank it to try to settle my stomach. Because of that, I didn't drink much water during the game. Anyway I came out of the huddle cramping. We had a time out and the trainer came out. I told him to give me water because I was cramping. He said, "Pinch your upper lip with your thumb and index finger and squeeze." There were supposed to be nerves there that released tension in your legs. I came out of the huddle limping and pinching my lip. I'll bet the cornerback thought, "This guy isn't going to catch any passes. They're not going to throw to him."

We got a quick touchdown on a ball I caught in the end zone. Danny scrambled and pointed for everybody to go to the left. I stayed where I was. Danny saw that, pumped, and drilled me in the end zone. That got us at least one touchdown away. We kicked off, held them, and got the ball back with two minutes left in the game. I was cramping, still pinching my lip, and it was working. It released tension in my legs to ease those cramps. I caught the final touchdown of the game on a post pattern. It was a blitz situation. Danny read it and I knew he was coming to me. He threw it before I broke and when I looked back, the ball was right there, and I caught it. I ended up catching those two touchdowns in the final four minutes to help us win that game and go to the NFC Championship. Through all the interviews when asked how I had done it, I said, "I had a guardian angel looking after me. That's how I did it. "

We won that game, 30-27 and went to Philadelphia the next week for the NFL Championship. We got handled pretty well and lost 20-7. Wilbur Montgomery ran all over us and we couldn't get anything going offensively. Consequently the Eagles went to the Super Bowl where they lost to the Oakland Raiders.

That 1980 season was dedicated to my Dad. It would have been great to climax it with a Super Bowl win. We didn't get that. But to be able to do what I did in the playoff game ....., I knew my Dad was a part of it.

In **1981** we won the NFC Eastern Division and beat Tampa Bay 38-0 in the first play-off game in Tampa Bay's franchise history. We moved on to face the San Francisco 49ers for the NFC

Championship. We led 10-7 after the first quarter on a 26-yard White-to-Hill touchdown pass. Joe Montana then hit Dwight Clark with a 20-yard touchdown to give the 49ers the lead. We took a 17-14 lead into halftime on a five-yard touchdown by Tony Dorsett. San Francisco came back to lead 21-17 after three quarters. With five minutes left in the game, Danny hit Doug Cosbie for a 21-yard touchdown to give us a 27-21 lead. Montana and the 49ers started their last drive from their 10-yard line and moved down the field. On a third down play, Montana scrambled to avoid the rush of Too Tall Jones. He rolled to his right and found Dwight Clark in the end zone for the game winning score with 51 seconds left to play. 'The Catch', as the play become known, started San Francisco's rise to supremacy in the 1980's while it marked the end of our reign. It was the last time I let a football game make me cry.

Charlie Waters and D.D. Lewis retired before the **1982** season. After two games we were 1-1 and the players went on strike.

The strike year was tough. It was hard for us to make the commitment to strike because we weren't making much money and needed the income. It was a tremendous sacrifice. We missed eight games because of the strike — eight weeks of pay.

We needed to do something to supplement our income. At the same time, we needed to stay in shape. Marques Haynes, my father-in-law, knew that we were available. Ron Springs and I played a couple of times with Marques' Harlem Magicians basketball team when they came to Texas. When Marques called and said, "We'd love to have you, Ron, and Tony Hill come go on the road with us," we agreed to go.

We were excited for a number of reasons. Number one, we

could make some money. Number two, we got to hang with and travel with Marques Haynes and the Harlem Magicians. Marques had uniforms made for us, and we became part of the team.

Our first game, we went to Rock Island, Illinois. We flew to Chicago and Marques picked us up and we drove to Rock Island. We got there the night before the game and thought, *Hey! The game's not until tomorrow evening so we'll sleep all day and get some rest.* We checked in, went to bed, and at 7:00 the next morning, Marques called our rooms. He didn't let his players lie around and do nothing all day. He had us in malls doing autograph sessions, visiting schools and doing radio interviews to promote the game. We were busy all day long. When game time came, it was a relief to get a break.

It was a great experience. The Globetrotters were famous for doing their circle routine before the game. They made a circle at center court, passed the ball through their legs, behind their backs and without looking. That was also part of the Harlem Magicians' act. Marques told me, "Drew, you get in the circle."

I said, "Marques, I don't know what to do. I'll get hit on the head or something. I won't know where the ball is coming from."

He said, "You just follow us and when the ball comes to you, you just pass it back to somebody."

They did the routine with music (*Rock Around the Clock*) and danced as they passed through their legs and behind their backs. Every time the ball came to me, I threw it right back to someone else. It looked like I was part of the routine. It was pretty cool, because most of the fans in Rock Island, or as they used to call it, The Rock, were football fans. They knew Drew Pearson because I had been in the NFL for years. They knew Tony Hill and Ron Springs. It was a thrill for me to be able to participate in that circle before the game and not mess it up.

When we got in the lay up line, all of the Magicians dunked the basketball and there we were doing our conventional lay ups. Hill could dunk, but his knees were bad. Springs couldn't dunk because he was a 235-pound fullback. Of course, I couldn't dunk. I could have used a chair. Where was Scotty when I needed him?

We had one white guy. I don't know where Marques found him but this kid could jump higher than anyone on the team. He was only about 5'10" and jumped out the gym. I couldn't believe this puny kid dunked like he did. He turned out to be the star of the game. To be a small white guy among all of those big African-American players helped make him a standout. They would set him up on a fast break and he did reverse jams, windmills and all of that good stuff.

We traveled with Marques for about four weeks and it gave me a chance to observe how Marques handled his business with the Magicians. Marques is a master at dealing with people. I think that many things I do today date from lessons I learned from Marques about how to deal with people.

We had a guy on the team called Big George (George Bell), who was 7'9". He wore a size 20 shoe. We once played a game in a small gym and the crowd was riding us hard. The other team got a little fired up so we tried to cool the atmosphere by making it a non-competitive game. One thing Marques incorporated into the game was that we would line up in a football formation. Marques was the quarterback. Tony and I acted like wide receivers and Marques kicked the ball to us like it was a pass. One time Marques kicked the ball to Hill. George Bell, in the fastest I ever saw him move, took off after Tony and tackled him on the court. We got huge laughs, but had to convince Marques not to make this part of the act. We thought we were going to play football again and didn't want Bell taking anybody out and make them miss the rest of the season.

Marques played with us and that became part of the pleasure of the situation. He played three quarters of a four-quarter game. He usually sat out the second quarter. He was still the attraction. I was impressed because I didn't think he would play that much. I figured he'd mostly coach and do P.R., but he went through his paces just like us. He played every game and when he broke into his dribbling act, the crowd was awed.

Marques never revealed his age, but he had to be in his 50's, yet he played effectively. He had a deadly half-court set shot. You saw him before the game practicing that shot, swooshing the net as he banked it off the glass. I said, "O.K. That's great, but I bet he can't do that in the game." Well, many times I saw him do it in a game. I saw him kick the ball into the basket from mid-court. I saw him bounce the ball from half-court into the basket. He did amazing things. Even though we were professionals, we were in awe of Marques Haynes, the legendary dribbler, Harlem Globetrotter, and Harlem Magician. It was a thrill and we cherished every moment. As a matter of fact, when the strike ended and it was time to play football again, we were a little disappointed. We had to leave the road and get back to the grind of playing football. Some of us made more money playing with Marques than we did playing pro football.

We did go back to football, however. Eight games were cancelled and because of the stoppage, the NFL devised a different playoff format for that year. The top eight teams in each conference made the playoffs and were seeded 1 through 8 with the number 1 seed playing the 8th seed, the 2nd seed playing the 7th and so on. We finished second to the Redskins.

We defeated Tampa Bay 30-17 in the first round and the Green Bay Packers 37-26 in round two. That set up the NFL Championship Game matching us with Washington. The Redskins were loaded on offense with Joe Theismann at quarterback, John Riggins at running back and a wide receiving corps called The Smurfs. Washington also had a great defense and won the game 31-17 to advance to the Super Bowl.

We got defensive end Jim Jeffcoat from Arizona State in the **1983** draft and won a wild card berth in the playoffs. The final two games of the year were a sign of things to come, however. In the final home game of the year, the Redskins beat us 31-10. Followed by a season-ending 42-17 drubbing in San Francisco.

Danny threw three interceptions and the Los Angeles Rams defeated us 24-17 in the first round of the play offs. After the season, Clint Murchison, Jr. sold the Cowboys to H.R. "Bum" Bright.

TRAGEDY

CHAPTER TWENTY-FOUR

★★★★★

One of the hardest things I've done in my life was to be married. It takes compromise to make a marriage work. I think the key is communication. That was the problem between Marsha and me. It wasn't a problem in the sense of her not communicating with me; it was the opposite. This caused us to grow apart and it was my fault. All of a sudden, at the age of 22, I went from Tulsa to starting wide receiver for Dallas Cowboys. A lot of temptations came my way. Sometimes they were hard to resist and it got to the point that I was doing things by myself that Marsha and I had previously done together. I would tell her, "I'll be back," and I didn't include her.

We separated for a short time in 1976. Then we separated again before the 1977 season and I moved in with Harvey Martin. It was serious the second time

Initially, the only person I talked to about the divorce and separation and the things I was experiencing was Harvey. Harvey was my best friend and he never offered any advice but he always listened.

Marsha is a wonderful person. She has a great personality. That was one of the things that attracted me to her in the first place. She is a beautiful lady. Her personality is outgoing and I thought she was a perfect fit for me because I am more of an introvert. People find it hard to believe but that's how I am. I've always been that way. I do what is necessary publicly because of the situation or circumstances, but I'm more reluctant to be around people than most who know me realize.

I wanted to make the marriage work and I know Marsha did. There's no question about it. If it was going to work, it was up to me. Living the bachelor life with Harvey through that season made me a bit irresponsible. I had a problem getting to meetings on time and my eating habits suffered. I stayed out late because I didn't have anything to tie me down. Tori, my oldest daughter, was three years old then. I went to see her but my visits were awkward.

Marsha and I started talking and decided to try to make our marriage work. I was kind of torn. I didn't know if I wanted to get back with her or stay where I was. In my mind, it was like playing tennis. I was lobbing back and forth. The main reason I struggled so much was that I didn't want to be a failure. I did not want to have divorce associated with my name. I did not want that to be associated with my family, even though my father and mother were divorced. I felt that it was a sign of failure. I felt I would be letting a lot of people down. Eventually I thought, *Hey, I've got to try to make this work.*

At the end of the 1977 season, everything was going well. We made it to the playoffs and went to the Super Bowl. I invited Marsha to the Super Bowl. I told Harvey and he said, "Good! You need to do that and try to work it out." The best thing he said was that she deserved it because she was a big part of my success. She made sacrifices in order for me to make it. She'd fought her family. Her mother in particular gave her a hard time, but she never wavered. She stayed with me and she supported me. She deserved to be there and be part of that experience.

She came to the Super Bowl and we got back together. Our reunion lasted another five years. The best thing about it was that we had our second daughter, Britni. But eventually, the communication wasn't there and we continued to grow apart. It got to the point where a decision had to be made. I told her before I went to training camp in 1983 that I wasn't coming back home. With the pressure of training camp and the final breakup of my marriage, I had a lot to deal with. We talked on the phone to see if anything could be done, but I told her this was the way it was going to be. I made the decision.

It got to the point in our relationship where we argued too often. I didn't want to continue something like that and she deserved better.

We went through training camp and when Coach Landry asked if anybody needed rooms at the hotel next to the Cowboys offices on Central Expressway, I raised my hand. The team proceeded to do a double take realizing I was on my own. I stayed there when we got back from training camp. This was where we had our meetings and housed the rookies. It was the headquarters hotel for the Cowboys through the rest of the preseason.

I visited the kids regularly when I got home. The first thing I did after we broke camp and I settled in the hotel was go talk to my children. They were young but I needed to explain the situation to them. It was difficult and emotional. They cried and hugged me and said "Daddy, don't go." But I'd made up my mind that this was the best thing for all of us.

Marsha filed for divorce because I wasn't living a saint's life. There was only so much she could stand. It was never a bitter thing and

I didn't want it to be. Many people didn't know we were going through this situation because I've always kept my personal life private. Of course, the media attention back then wasn't like it is today. We did a few family articles together but that was it. I took my kids to the autograph sessions and hung out with them at games but that was as much exposure as they got to fans and the public. Nobody knew the particulars about our family because I made a conscientious effort to keep it private.

I talked about it often with Jay Saldi. I remember telling Jay, "I want this to work. I feel I'm letting down so many people by getting a divorce. It seems like the easy way out. I can't imagine telling Roger Staubach that I'm divorced. I can't imagine telling Tom Landry that I'm getting a divorce."

Jay said, " You can't worry about those people. I know you respect them but you can't worry about them. You've got to make decisions based on what you think is right and best for Drew and the people your decision is going to affect."

I thought about that piece of advice and he was right. Marsha filed for divorce and I didn't contest it. She got a high-priced attorney, and of course, I had to pay for all of that. She hired attorneys who were known as tough negotiators. I had Mel Cline, a Highland Park attorney and I paid him big money. We went back and forth all through the season. As it turned out my last season in the NFL ended with a 24-17 wild card playoff loss to the LA Rams

To that point, I had played out my first contract from beginning to end. I renegotiated the others to raise my salary to a respectable level for a starter. My third year, I earned as much as Billy Joe Dupree who was the No. 1 draft choice the year I came into the league. That was a major goal for me. Billy Joe never knew he provided that inspiration for me.

The Cowboys wanted me back. David Falk was my agent. He was famous as the agent for Michael Jordan. Falk was with a company called Pro Serve. The Cowboys made an initial offer of $400,000 and we came back with a counter offer of $600,000 per season. I wanted to get this negotiation and divorce behind me so I went to the office of Mel Cline and told him, "Let's get this done."

He asked me, "What do you mean?"

I said, "I'm ready to give up everything. Whatever Marsha wants, she gets." I gave up virtually everything, the bank accounts, the house, the cars and all of the furniture in the house. I also paid for all the attorney fees. But I did so with the stipulation that there would be no coming back for more. I even agreed to what I considered to be a generous alimony and child support payments because I felt that I still had earning power and I knew that potentially I had this big contract. We hoped to get at least a half a million dollars per football season.

I knew I had a lot of earning power so I wanted to get this deal done quickly. It was a sad moment when we settled. Marsha wasn't the only one who cried. I cried as we negotiated. However, I felt somewhat at peace because I felt that it was the best thing for us to do, the best thing for our children.

CHAPTER TWENTY-FIVE

★★★★★

My brother Carey was the smallest child in our family but we called him "Moose". I'm not sure how he got the name. When he got out of high school, he had aspirations of going to college and playing ball. However, he was having difficulty in his personal life. He got his girlfriend pregnant and had to deal with that so I helped move him to Dallas. He brought his family and I helped them rent an apartment.

He stayed a short while, then moved back to New Jersey. When I got divorced I moved into an apartment at the Prestonwood Country Club and Moose came back to Dallas and lived with me. I tried to help him out by finding him some work.

Moose was like many of us Pearsons. We want to do things our way. We don't want a hand out. Moose didn't want a hand out. As a kid growing up and going through high school, there was always pressure on him to live up to his brothers' accomplishments. Even though he was a good high school football player, I don't think people gave him enough credit or respect because they didn't think he was as good as me. I think that was hard for Moose to accept and I understood. That was part of his problem. I think the other part was that he had to grow up fast. Having a child at such a young age burdened him with a heavy responsibility.

Moose helped me with the Dallas Cowboys basketball team. I was the manager, coach, negotiator, promoter and sometimes the bus driver. I started the team my second year in the league. The Cowboys organization frowned on it because they'd had problems in the past with their players playing basketball. I went to Tex Schramm and convinced him that we would do it right; promote the Cowboys and not do anything to hurt the name. I told him that it would be a bonus for the Cowboys as far as the exposure we would get in the off-season. He gave me his blessing to do it. I did it and I did it up big.

We played about 40 games in a two-month period. The players earned anywhere from $200 to $500 per game, depending on where we played or how many players we had. Some of the guys who played every game made more money playing basketball than they did as NFL football players. Often I called them to play and their wives said, "He's not here right now, but he'll go."

I always played and Moose helped me manage. He did everything from washing uniforms to making sure the balls had air. I think he found something he enjoyed. The guys liked him and he enjoyed being around them. I could tell that he did because he opened up to me more. He talked more. I was quiet, but Moose was extremely introverted.

We went to Coalgate, Oklahoma, to play a charity game. The guys made $250 each. We had a bus and met at the old practice field on Forest Lane. We had a nice ride on a beautiful day. The gym was filled and the fans were pumped up. We made money, the charity made money, and the promotion came off as a huge success.

We drove back from Coalgate late because we didn't leave until after ten. We always had a good time on the bus. The guys would have a few beers on the bus. The big thing, however, was to play cards. I usually didn't play, but this time, I played poker and smoked them. I won like crazy. I took all of Doug Donley's game check. He went to Coalgate, Oklahoma, for nothing.

We got back to the practice field and the guys were glad to get home so they left quickly. I reminded them that we were leaving the next day for Virginia and a three-game basketball series with the Washington Redskins. We were going to play two games in Virginia and one in D.C.

I was excited about winning the poker game and only had a couple of beers on the bus. I planned to give the poker money to Moose as an extra bonus. After all of the guys left, Moose and I cleaned the bus. We took the trash out, unloaded the uniforms and put them in the car. Since I was leaving town, I was going to take Moose to my brother Andre's house. He had moved from New Jersey, and he and his wife, Gina were living in Garland. Moose was going to stay with them for the weekend.

I had a promotion deal with Summers Chrysler/Dodge in Redbird. My compensation was a car to drive. The only car I'd ever gotten from them was a luxury class 5th Avenue, New Yorker. Before we left for Coalgate that day I went to the dealer and traded my 5th Avenue for a black Dodge Daytona. The Dodge had a sunroof and it was beautiful. I told Charlie Rains, the general manager, "Charlie, I want that car. Let me drive that for a while."

He said, "Are you sure? That's not your style. That's a five speed. You know you don't like a stick shift."

I said, "But it's so cool, man. Let me drive it for a couple of weeks. If I don't like it, I'll bring it in and switch back to the New Yorker."

He said, "O.K."

The new wheels were a hot-running sports model. This was what we drove to the practice field. Moose and I loaded the Daytona with the equipment and coolers and drove toward Garland on 635. It was amazing how everything unfolded because most of it is blank. I remember getting on the freeway and going east up the ramp. We only had to go a few exits. That's all I remember. The next thing I remembered was waking up in the mangled car with lights blinking all around. My brother's head was lying on my shoulder. I was groggy as I shook Moose and thought, *Oh God. There's an accident? How did an accident happen?"* When I shook my brother, he was limp and I wondered, *Is he dead?*

I leaned my brother against the window and got out of the car. The paramedics were stunned. They came rushing and grabbed me. I said, "What happened… What happened?" There was glass all over the highway. I saw that traffic was stopped. I saw all of the cop cars, and I said again, "What happened?"

They said, " You ran into an eighteen wheeler that was parked on the side of the road." When you go through a car accident, there is usually screeching of tires, the throwing up of hands, or the grabbing of the steering wheel to brace yourself for impact. I don't remember any of that. It was like I had been spiritually removed from the car and put back in. Moose was taken out and *not* put back in. The paramedics explained to me what had happened, and then the cops started talking to me. I had a lacerated liver, broken clavicle, and the stick shift had punctured my thigh. They put me in the ambulance.

I asked them, "Is my brother dead?" They told me he was and I went into shock. The last thing I remember hearing as they put me in the ambulance was, "You know we're going to have to give you the

Breathalyzer." Then I passed out. A Breathalyzer was the last thing I was worrying about. My brother was dead.

At the hospital, my liver was hemorrhaging and I was trying to hold on. In my sedated state all I could think about was that my mom and my brothers and sisters probably knew about the accident and that my brother was dead. I was lying in Presbyterian Hospital in Dallas fighting for my life. At the same time, my family was trying to deal with the devastation of losing my brother.

Having lived on that curve in South River on Prospect Street, car accidents were something I had grown up around. We had seen many accidents. I also had a good friend who was killed on Route 18 after getting out of the Navy. Back then there were frequent accidents on Route 18. Our family was familiar with accidents but none had happened to us.

My family went through the experience of burying Moose. After they laid my brother to rest, they flew to Dallas to comfort me. Meanwhile, I was sedated from surgeries and testing. Every time I was moved or turned, I saw three people. Actually I only saw their blurred images. I couldn't speak, touch, or reach out but I knew those three people were Tom Landry, Roger Staubach and Harvey Martin.

Later, after I was transferred to a private room, I reflected on their vigils. I expected Roger and Harvey to be there, but I had never expected Coach Landry. I had no idea that he cared that much about any of his players because of the way he presented himself. I thought he was calculated and remained aloof from players in order to demand their respect. I realized later while coaching with him that he was concerned and compassionate about all of his players and that he agonized when he had to cut someone.

I found out later that he was there constantly. He was present when my family arrived. He comforted them, he prayed with them and he consoled them. Even more amazing is that he did this during a mini-camp. Mini-camp took place the weekend after the accident. This was during mini-camp time, a critical period as we progressed toward the 1984 season.

I was hurting physically and mentally. I couldn't believe the accident happened. I was wracked with guilt. I had taken my brother away from my family and to this day I still feel the guilt. I can't forgive myself for what happened. Maybe it was something beyond my control, but still it happened. It felt as though I had control to prevent it from happening. The gap from entering the freeway to waking up after the accident still bothers me. What happened? Was I joking or messing around? Were we arguing? Did I turn? Did I lose control because it was that sports car — fast and powerful with a stick shift. Was I having a problem with the clutch? All of those things go through my mind as possible reasons and I can't find peace. It's amazing how one block of time was eliminated from my memory and I can't get it back. I guess I'll get that answer somewhere down the road. It certainly won't be answered by any of us mortals. But in due time, maybe I'll get the answer as to why it happened, why I was spared when my brother's life was taken.

After the operation, they had trouble draining blood from my body. The doctor came in and said, "We're going to have to insert a tube."

I asked, "Where?" I thought it would be through my nose or throat.

The doctor said, "No, we're going to have to put it through your side, near your liver."

I said, "What?"

The doctor explained further: "We'll crack two ribs and insert tubes to help it drain." They shot me with Demerol, and I was out, feeling no pain. They started the procedure. The doctor pressed my ribs until they snapped. I heard it despite being sedated. I could feel it. I never felt such excruciating pain in my life. I yelled, screamed, and cried. And that was just the first crack. They had to make two. They pressed, the second one popped and the same intense pain shot through me.

They got the tubes in me and were able to drain blood, which helped begin the healing process. My family was there the whole time. Coach Landry kept coming and so did the teammates. Some days I reached the point where I couldn't see anybody because the pain was so bad. I didn't want anyone to see me in that condition. I didn't want Coach Landry to see me hurting like that.

I still wear the scar today. With modern procedures, you can get scars removed or cosmetically redone, but I don't want to. Mine is a reminder of that situation – what I went through and the pain that it caused. I also have a scar under my pectorals, down through my navel from where they entered to do the surgery on my liver. Again, that's something you can get fixed. But I look at it every day to remind myself of what I went through.

When I left the hospital and went to my apartment, I still had family there and everyone tried to console me. I was mostly confined to the bed. I could do light walking exercises but it was painful. I was extremely sore for two weeks. It was agony merely to walk to the bathroom.

I thought about all of the things leading up to the accident, *Maybe if I hadn't taken that car. Maybe it was the black car.* I remember that day I had dressed in all black. The only thing white on me was the Adidas stripes on my pants. I had a black hat, shirt, shoes, and pants. I wondered, "Was that an omen?"

All of these things went through my mind. It weighed heavily on me. Layers and layers of depression descended on me. The only reason I was able to deal with it was my family. My mother, in particular, was a spiritual person. She comforted me in a motherly way and a spiritual way as well. She explained how we lost a loved one, and even though we lost him, we were lucky that I was alive, because losing us both would have been twice as devastating. She tried to put the tragedy in perspective from her relationship with God. It gave me comfort. My feelings of guilt were very, very strong. The mental part was more difficult to deal with than the physical. I knew I would get well physically in due time, but I wasn't sure I would ever heal mentally.

REBUILDING

CHAPTER TWENTY-SIX
★★★★★

My marriage ended in February of 1984. One month later on March 22, 1984, I had my car accident. I lost my brother and I was seriously injured. The injuries I sustained caused me to retire from the NFL. My last paycheck from the Cowboys came August 31, 1984.

All of a sudden, it was all gone. I didn't know what I would do. I had monthly child support payments and the house payments and everything was gone. This was a tremendous turn in a life where everything had gone smoothly and great things had happened. Now, within a six-month period, everything changed. The marriage was over, football was gone, my brother was dead, and my last paycheck was cashed.

It was devastating to me. I probably suffered from depression without knowing it, because back then that condition wasn't talked about much. There weren't many medications to deal with it. I could only imagine how my family felt when they got that dreaded phone call. As kids growing up, and as a parent, you dreaded getting that call at night that there'd been an accident.

Before the accident, Billy Joe Dupree said, "Everything Drew touches turns to gold." He was right until the divorce and the accident. It was a storybook type of life up until then. Those were major setbacks. Divorce made me feel I had failed as a person, husband and father. Then the accident a month later put me in a state of serious depression.

I was a mental wreck, I was retired from football and needed a job. I went to work for CBS Sports as a color analyst. They offered me eight games that season which was pretty good for a rookie analyst. Billy Sims of Detroit, tore up his knee in one of the games I covered. Sims ran a sweep to the right and didn't get hit that hard, but came up limping. He had to make it to his sideline. I was announcing the game, and I said, "It looks like he's going to be all right. I think it's just a twist or a sprain." It turned out to be a career-ending knee injury for Sims. The last game I did that season was the Battle of the Bays. It was Tampa Bay at Green Bay in December. It was really a nothing game. Nobody was going to the playoffs, but Packers fans didn't treat it that way. They reacted as if it was a championship game or the Super Bowl, despite below zero temperatures. This was the lowest rung of the broadcasting ladder for CBS. Nobody wanted to do this game so they threw me in there. It turned out to be my last game with CBS because the network didn't hire me the next year. After the season ended, Rudy Martze, who does USA Today's radio-TV column listed the top 10 analysts, I was number five. Then he named his pick for Rookie of the Year. I was the Rookie of the Year as an analyst. I beat out Terry Bradshaw and others, so I thought, "Great, this is my career now." I made $90,000, but I only had a one-year contract.

My agent, David Falk, called CBS to start negotiating a contract for the next year. CBS told Falk that they weren't interested and didn't want to bring me back. Of course David asked why and they said, "Well, he's not excitable enough. He's a product of the Landry School."

Falk asked, "What is that?'

They said, "He's just like the other Cowboys players that we've had attempt to be analysts. They certainly know the game, but they're not excitable enough; they're not the personality we're looking for."

Roger and Charlie Waters tried before me and they didn't last long, either. They lumped me with those guys. This was when John Madden made his mark as an announcer and he was what everyone was looking for, the boom, the bah type.

After CBS let me go, I tried to figure out what in the heck I was going to do. I felt good physically. I worked out and got in shape to the point where I thought about making a comeback. As a matter of fact, I said, "I'm going to make a comeback. If they don't want me to talk about the game, I'll give them something to talk about by playing in the game."

I went to the surgeon who repaired my liver after the accident. He checked me out thoroughly and said, "Drew, you're good to go." I had a hole in my liver the size of a grapefruit from the wreck. When I went back to him, the liver had regenerated and the hole had closed to the size of a quarter. Even though it wasn't completely filled, the surgeon said there was nothing threatening. He told me that even if I got hit directly on it and my liver started hemorrhaging again, it wasn't life threatening.

I was pumped and worked out harder. From my mother's house in Jersey, I called Tex Schramm, and when he got on the phone I said, "Tex, I want to make a comeback. I want to play again." I told him that my doctor had given me the O.K.

Tex was excited. He said, "Really? Can we get the x-rays?.. What kind of shape are you in?.. I'm sure Coach Landry wants to hear this."

My mom had been sitting there the whole time and as she heard my end of the conversation, she started getting excited because I had not told her that I was going to try to make a comeback.

Tex talked to Coach Landry and Coach Landry was for it 100%, but they both said they wanted another medical opinion. They sent x-rays and scans to a renowned liver specialist at the University of Pittsburgh, a pioneer in transplants. He checked my scans and x-rays and reported to the Cowboys. His conclusion was, "He can play again, but I can't give him 100% clearance. He's 99% healed."

Coach Landry and I talked about that. I told him, "It's got to be 100%. If I can't be the kind of player I was before I left the game, I don't want to tarnish what I had."

Coach Landry agreed. He said, "It's got to be 100%. As much as we need you, I care for you too much as a person and have too much respect for you and what you've done to settle for anything less than 100%." After talking about a half hour on the phone with Coach Landry, who was getting ready for the start of training camp, I came to the conclusion that he was right.

Before the conversation ended he said, "Why don't you come to training camp and work with the rookie receivers and see if you can help me get them ready. See if any of them are good enough to make the team."

The Cowboys were desperately looking for back-up receivers. They drafted Karl Powe from Alabama State, who was the spitting image of John Stallworth, and Leon Gonzales from Bethune-Cookman. There were others there, but Karl and Leon were the leading candidates to make the team. My job was to work with these two guys and get them ready to make the team.

I went from player to coach within a year. Playing was cool because when practice was over, you were practically done for the day. When you coached, however, when practice was over, the work started. I went from one meeting right after another and at 11 at night we were still working. Coaching was time consuming and I questioned whether it was what I wanted to do.

We completed training camp. I got those guys ready and they made the team. The four receivers were Mike Renfro, Tony Hill, Gonzales and Powe. During training camp I was earning $1,000 a week and I needed the money. After training camp broke and we got back to Dallas, Coach Landry called me in. He said, "You did a good job with these receivers. Would you like to stay on?"

I said, "Yeah, sure." I didn't have anything else to do and I always wanted to be in a front office position after I retired. I figured this would be my opportunity. I didn't want to be a coach forever. I saw this as perhaps the beginning of a career in management.

Coach Landry said, "We'd like to keep you on for the season. Your job is to work with those two rookie wide receivers and have them ready by mid-season in case I need them."

I said, "O.K. Coach."

I took Powe and Gonzales under my wing, and everything I did, they did. They followed me and I taught them how to run, how to catch and what they needed to do during pre game warm-up. I suppose I tried to have them emulate Drew Pearson. Coach Landry signed me as a coach for $60,000 and that was enough since I didn't have time to spend money anyway. I was mired there. I recall peeking into the office of defensive coordinator Ernie Stautner. He had a clothes rack, hot plate, microwave, refrigerator and a cot. I thought, *Man, I don't think this guy ever goes home.* Then I'd go by Jerry Tubbs' office and he had the same set-up. So did Dick Nolan, Jim Myers and the other assistants. It made me ask myself if that was where I really wanted to be in 10 years. I didn't think so.

The whole time I coached. I thought about something else. That was not for me. It was too confining. Marsha would call and there would be something wrong with the day-care center, but I couldn't go. If something happened at school, I couldn't leave. The only time Coach Landry ever let me leave practice was when the IRS called me to meet with them on a back taxes issue. I had to bring a note from the IRS agent saying that I was actually with him. It took an act of the U.S. government for Coach Landry to excuse me.

I complained to Nolan. Nolan told me, "Quit complaining Pearson. This is the coaching business and that's just the way it is. I've been doing this for thirty years."

I thought, *Yeah, that's what I don't want to be doing.*

I was a rookie coach. Staff meetings always started at 7:30 and I was always the last one there. I learned more football as a coach, but, because I was the rookie, I also learned how to make coffee and popcorn. I also learned how to smoke cigarettes, because some of the coaches smoked. I'd say, "Hey, give me one." I smoked cigarettes, drank coffee and ate popcorn all day. That's what we would eat - snacks. No one catered lunch, no one went out to get food, and no one complained.

The worst day was Tuesday because that was the players' day off and the day we put the game plan together. We had a staff meeting at 7:30 and sometimes I appeared wearing the same clothes I had on when I left the night before. We had only a few hours to have fun and I took advantage of it. I'd come rolling back in and Nolan would take a look at me, shake his head, and say, "You'll never make it. You'll never make it. You can't burn it at both ends Pearson, not in this business." He used to get on me all the time, but he did it out of love because he liked and respected me.

The staff meetings on Tuesdays were short so we could get the game plan together. The offensive and defensive coaches broke up to discuss which plays we would run. We graded films and tapes and then put the running game, the passing game, the play action, the deceptives, and the short yardage goal line plays together. We were there for hours. I sat there listening and trying to learn how to do it. Coach Landry came by every so often to stick his head in the door and say "Are you ready for me?"

We'd say, "No, no, we're not ready yet."

By mid-afternoon, we'd have what we thought was the game plan. The group included Jim Shofner, Jim Myers, a legendary offensive line coach who had been with the Cowboys for 30 years, Dick Nolan, former head coach with the Saints and 49ers who had taken the 49ers to a Championship Game and played with Coach Landry in New York, and Al Lavan who was the running back coach. This group must have put a million game plans together, but they were still intimidated to present what they had come up with to Coach Landry. There was a good reason for that.

When Coach Landry came in, he sat at the head of the table. Everyone would have his head down. No one made eye contact with him. Shofner, who was the coordinator, would go to Coach Landry with his head down and say, "Here's what we came up with."

We sat there thinking, *Oh God.*

The next thing we knew, Landry had his pen out marking things off and saying, "We can't run this… We can't run that… What made you think we could run this?" He tore up everything. Then he went to the board and said, "Here's what we're going to do." He laid out the game plan, bam, bam, bam, bam.

We'd think, *Yeah, why didn't we think of that?*

Then he'd say, "O.K.," and leave the room. It happened like that for 16 straight weeks.

He went to the defense and did the same thing. While it took us seven or eight hours to come up with something, Coach Landry studied the film in his office. Then he laid out the game plan in thirty minutes. These coaches with all of their NFL experience were in awe. It was unbelievable. But that's how Coach Landry was. He knew his stuff. We sat there and shook our heads over what we had just witnessed

We had a good season and made the playoffs. We played the Rams in Anaheim, California. Eric Dickerson ran for a playoff record 248 yards and we lost 20-0. Before the game, I was probably more "up" than most players because it was a playoff game. It didn't matter that I was coaching; I was fired up for it. I didn't see any intensity in the players, however, and that was frustrating to me.

After the season ended, I let Coach Landry know that coaching wasn't for me. I realized mid-way through that season that it was not what I wanted to do. Ken Shead and Mike Russell had approached me about going into the sports apparel business with them. They had been trying to convince me for almost a year to join them. They worked as sales representatives for Xerox and the Sperry Corporation. They were top sales people but were tired of making all of that money for someone else. They wanted to make money for themselves by starting a business.

It was a recruiting effort on their part. My brother Andre worked with Shead at Xerox and I got to know him through Andre. Ken and

Mike took me to dinners to convince me to go into business with them. I kept turning them down. They even let me play on the Sperry Corporation basketball team every Wednesday night. In basketball, all I did was shoot. I'm a gunner. I don't play defense. If I'm hot, we're in good shape, but if I'm cold, forget it. Most of the time I was cold, but these guys kept letting me shoot anyway.

About half way through that season as a coach I contacted them and said, "Hey, Let's do it!" They were gung ho and ready to go. They quit their jobs immediately. We started what was known then as Drew Pearson Enterprises. Our first office was Shead's kitchen. Our first business cards had Shead's home address and phone number on them. That's how we started Drew Pearson Marketing. While I finished out the rest of that football season, these guys began cultivating business.

A good friend of mine, Gary Delaune, a TV legend in San Antonio and the state of Texas, had been doing reports in Dallas on the Cowboys. He knew that I had aspirations of getting into the TV business. He asked if I was interested in becoming a weekend sports anchor in San Antonio. I said, "Yes, of course!" We worked it out and during, the summer of 1986, I got the job as weekend sportscaster for KENS TV, a CBS affiliate and the number one station in San Antonio.

When I met with Coach Landry he tried to talk me into staying on as a coach. He convinced me to stay on as a scout for senior college wide receivers. The Cowboys were interested in drafting a wide receiver as their number one pick in the 1986 draft, so I scouted all week long and then went to San Antonio as the weekend sportscaster. At the same time, I was trying to start up this new business. I also had a job with HBO Sports doing feature reports for their "Inside the NFL" show. I went around the country filing reports on the players and what they did with their lives away from football.

There was no way I could continue to do it all. I got through the scouting period for the Cowboys. They made their choice and they drafted Mike Sherrard of UCLA as their number one pick. Much of their decision was based on my advice and references. Then after about six months of doing the weekend job in San Antonio, that job got to me, too. I resigned. The only thing I did then was HBO and Drew Pearson Enterprises.

The HBO opportunity was satisfying and I ended up doing it for three years. I liked traveling to the different NFL cities and visiting with NFL players. I remember going to Minnesota to do a story on Joey Browner of the Vikings. We interviewed Browner on the field and had to wait until the team came out of a meeting. The crew and I were on the practice field throwing the ball around. I was snagging balls with one hand, all sweet like a wide receiver. I was a couple of years removed from the game, so I was still in shape. I didn't realize that the Minnesota coaches were in their offices, looking down on the field from their windows. They kept saying, "Who's that guy down there catching the football?" They came down to the field for the practice and said, "Oh, that's Drew Pearson. No wonder he's catching that ball." They asked if I had any eligibility left. They told me, "You catch better than anybody we've got out here."

In the meantime, we were working with Drew Pearson Marketing. We got a $20,000 loan from the bank and that allowed us to move into an executive office complex. We needed more money to make the business work. We set a goal for ourselves to raise $100,000 by selling debentures for the business at $25,000 each and were able to raise the funds. We raised $75,000 in a relatively short period of time and our final presentation was to Roger Staubach. We never took the connection and friendship between Roger and me for granted because we knew this was business. I certainly didn't want Roger to invest in something just because it was Drew Pearson's. I wanted him to invest in something that was solid and that he felt comfortable with. We made a full-blown presentation and Roger was quite impressed with it. He wrote us a check for $25,000, which was the final piece of the $100,000 we needed to raise.

In spite of raising $100,000, we had some lean times. We made bad business decisions and by the early part of 1987 we were nearly broke. Roger came through for us again and let us office at the old Cowboys practice field.

This was the same field where I had gone for 11 years to practice, work out, and get ready for the season. The Cowboys had moved to Valley Ranch, so the field was vacant. Roger's real estate company owned options to buy the property. By owning the options, he controlled the property. They weren't doing anything with it and it was an eyesore sitting there on Forest Lane. We met with Roger and told him that we would improve the property if he would let us office there. What better place for Drew Pearson Marketing to office than the old Cowboys practice field?

Roger was so generous; he let us office there with no rent. Bob Breunig, a former teammate, was working for Roger at the time. He came by to collect the rent and I said, "Yeah, yeah, yeah, Bob. We'll take care of it." As soon as Bob left, I phoned Roger to tell him Bob had been over there to see us.

Roger said, "I'll take care of it. Don't worry about it." For the three years that we stayed there, we never paid one dime of rent. When you're a start-up business and can eliminate an expense like that, that's big. The trade out was that we fixed up the property and maintained it.

We cut the grass, upgraded the look on the outside, painted the building, and turned the front into "The Old Cowboys Locker Room Store" where we sold Cowboys merchandise. We had the old lockers there and when people came into town for Cowboys games we became a stop on their schedule. If they bought something it gave them the right to tour the facility. We changed things out to make the locker room look like an office, but it was still the locker room. It still had the showers, the saunas, the training room, and the old cage where Buck Buchanan kept the equipment. Some of the lockers remained in place and the carpet was the same. People came into town to buy something, and were excited to take the tour of the Cowboys practice field.

We made some money with the store, which helped our cash flow, but soon we were in dire straights. We were out of money again. We didn't know if we could borrow from the bank or if we should approach the investors for more money. But here came another Hail Mary.

I got a call from ABC Sports. It was an opportunity to compete in the Veteran Superstar competition. They sent me a list of the players who were competing. There were guys like John Havlicek, Walt Frazier, and Jerry Koosman and I thought, *Man, these guys are old. I grew up watching them.* I looked at the list and I was the youngest entry. So I called them and said, "Yeah, I'll compete." This was our chance to raise money. The top prize for the winner of the competition was $25,000. I told my partners I could win it.

I came into work early every day and trained at the old practice field. I ran sprints and laps around the field just like I did back in the days when I was playing for the Cowboys. After I worked out, I showered in the old locker room. Sometimes when I was sore, I sat in the sauna. When it was time to compete, I was in shape and ready. I was psyched up and motivated to win the contest because we needed the prize money to keep our business going.

The first day of competition, I won bowling, basketball shooting, and all of the other competitions. The only way I could lose was if I faltered on the second day. The second day was mostly running events. There was the 100-yard dash, half mile run, obstacle course, and the bike race. I won them all. Joe Torre was one of the competitors. He walked the 800 and I lapped him. There were some great athletes there but I was so much younger that I dominated the competition.

That night when I got back to my hotel, I hardly celebrated because I was so sore. I ended up ordering a bottle of champagne from room service and celebrated by myself. They gave me a bowl for winning the competition along with the check for $25,000. I poured the bottle of champagne into the bowl and drank the champagne. I spoke with Ken and Mike on the phone and told them I won. They were excited and couldn't wait until I got back – not to see me, but to get that money, I'm sure.

I invested all of that money into the company and it kept the doors open another three months.

The business started working and we began to figure out the best way to maneuver it. We discovered that the way to do it in the sports apparel business was through licensing to entities like the NFL, Major League Baseball, the Olympics, and colleges. What we decided to do was to list the most prolific licensing agreements, target them and go after them. We listed 10 licensing agreements like the pro sports leagues, colleges, Coca Cola, Disney, Warner Brothers and groups like that. Then we devised a plan of attack to go after these licensing opportunities.

The first one we went after was the United States Olympic Committee. This was in connection with the Games of 1988. The 1984 Games were held in Los Angeles so there was much carryover interest about the '88 Olympics. We made presentations to the United States Olympic Committee and shortly after that, got a call from the Committee chairman. He asked if we could come to Colorado Springs to sign an agreement with the Committee. He said, "We're giving you exclusive headwear rights in conjunction with the 1988 Olympics."

We were ecstatic. There must have been 200 companies bidding on the contract. They were all more qualified, more experienced, and more established in the industry, but we got the license. We could not believe we had won over of all those big companies. Probably one of the big reasons we got it was that the Olympic Committee was looking for a minority company to associate with. They would have been under pressure if they had out-sourced all their business without minority companies listed.

We slapped fives and congratulated ourselves. But, after speaking with the Olympic Committee, we said, "Now what do we do?" We didn't know where to take this because it was big. The contract was huge. It controlled all the headwear rights for retail and corporate sponsors that wanted to associate their logos with the United States Olympic Committee's five rings logo. This was a tremendous undertaking and we didn't know what to do. We didn't have any sourcing connections even though we had put all of that in our proposal.

After we got those rights, companies we had beat out started calling trying to get involved with the Olympic Committee through us. We thought, *This is not a bad way to go.* We weeded out most calls and settled on a company called Promotional Headwear out of Lenexa, Kansas. We worked out a deal with them to help us service the Olympic agreement. They had the sourcing connections, money, experience in the field, connections at retail, and they knew about the premium business. It was a natural for us to associate with them. Doing that infused capital into our company.

That was our first opportunity, and it gave us instant credibility in the industry. All of a sudden, we were associated with the United States Olympic Committee. People were starting to take notice of Drew Pearson Enterprises. This gave us confidence to pursue the rest of the licensing agreements on our list.

The next one we went after was Disney. The first time we met with Disney, I could tell that the guy was laughing under his breath. We were not prepared and got slapped down and ridiculed. We didn't present the proper information and our dialogue wasn't right. But instead of laughing and brushing us off, they referred us to the minority and diversity program associated with Disney. Through that program, we learned how to set up and present proposals.

After three months of training, we approached Disney again and this time we were better prepared. Our presentation was much more polished and professional. Disney was impressed because they saw where we had come from and what we had achieved. We were now a product of Disney's diversity and minority program. Because of that, we now had some momentum. Disney granted us the licensing rights to use their mouse and logos on golf hats. This was a small niche category, but it was an opportunity to get in the door with Disney.

At the same time we worked with Disney, we also approached the NFL and other professional sports leagues. The NFL turned us down. We couldn't even get a meeting with them. I finally convinced them to let us come to New York to make a presentation and when we got there it was like talking to a wall. All I can remember was their final statement. They said, "We gave O.J. Simpson a license and he couldn't do anything with it. What makes you think you're going to do something with it."

I told them, "I don't know what that situation was with O.J., but if you give us an opportunity, we'll show you what we can do with it."

When I left that meeting, I told Ken and Mike. "If we get this opportunity, we're going to make this work because they're not going to be able to tell that same story to the next former player or the next African-American that tries to get a license." We didn't, however, get the license.

Late in 1987, Al Campanis of the Los Angeles Dodgers made negative statements about African-Americans in sports. He said that their skills were more suitable for the playing field than the front office or coaching positions. Almost before the words came out of his mouth, reaction was all over the wires and Ted Koppel was reporting it on Nightline.

Campanis was forced to resign because of his remarks and the situation prompted the Reverend Jesse Jackson to organize his Fairness in Athletics Committee. When I got word that the committee was being formed, I contacted Rev. Jackson's office and told them that we wanted to be involved. Reverend Jackson was concerned about having more African-Americans in coaching and front office positions in the NFL. I convinced him that they needed to add African-Americans doing business with the pro sports leagues to their agenda. We found that of the 300 or so companies with NFL licenses, not one was an African-American company and not one was associated with a former player.

We had a brief meeting with Reverend Jackson and his committee in Chicago at the first Fairness in Athletics meeting. Reverend Jackson already had the Rainbow Coalition set up to deal with inequities in the business world through major corporations. Our idea was to branch off of that.

Mike, Ken and I had the opportunity to meet with Reverend Jackson to tell him our story. He said, "We're going to give you a chance to talk at a press conference and you can bring that up." We went into a ballroom packed with media representatives. There were cameras, lights, and photographers snapping pictures.

I stood at the podium with Reverend Jackson. I was impressed with his influence. Maybe that power has dwindled over time, but back then, when he spoke, people listened. I stood there with Reverend Jackson and others associated with him and I felt powerful. One person made a presentation about coaches. He gave all the numbers and facts and spoke about the inequities on the coaching side. Another talked about the front office as far as general managers, presidents and owners of teams were concerned. Finally it was my turn to talk about the lack of associations that the league had with minority businesses.

I made a five-minute presentation and I think I was thoroughly convincing. At first I was a bit nervous because I didn't want to embarrass myself in front of Reverend Jackson. We were prepared. I had facts and laid them out. The final point was that it would take time to move minorities into coaching and management positions but doing business with African-Americans was something the pro leagues could do immediately.

After my presentation and the press conferences were over, a representative from Major League Baseball came up to me and asked, "When can you come to New York? When can we sit down and talk?"

Baseball was the sport getting the most criticism from the fallout over Campanis' statement. Baseball wanted to do something immediately. We went to New York, and ended up coming out of there with a baseball license.

From there the NFL started listening to us and taking us a little more seriously. We went to New York and they granted us a license. It was what they called "the golf cap category," which was baseball hats that had to have the leather strap in the back to make it look like a golf cap. It wasn't really what we wanted, but we took it.

Two weeks later they called us back to New York. We didn't have a lot of money to fly around. We were flying coach, stand-by, or whatever was the cheapest fare. When we traveled, instead of having individual hotel rooms, three of us stayed in the same room. I wasn't used to rooming with guys. What made it worse was that Ken snored terribly. I knew that the people next door heard him. I'm sure that even people down the hall could hear him, too. This guy was the worst. I ended up sleeping in the bathroom to get away from the snoring and get some rest.

We went to NFL Properties and met with Bob Carey, the president of NFL Properties. We sat at a conference table with several NFL Properties people. They began the meeting beating around the bush but finally got to their point. They wanted to take this golf cap category away from us and give us something else in headwear. We didn't understand why but apparently they felt pressure from someone for giving us this potentially big license. We argued with them and the talks went back and forth. Carey finally said, "We're reneging on the contract." We sat there stunned. He said, "We need that contract back and here's what we're going to give you in return." We were still in the NFL game and we had a little control. They were begging us for the license back. They took back the golf cap category, and in return, they gave us a regular headwear license. Now the license was for the "coaches cap" category. To us, it was much the same.

I know what the NFL did. They granted us the licensing rights to set us up for failure. They didn't have confidence that we could make this work. They figured that in a month or two we would disappear. We would be gone and they would be rid of us. Then they could say, "Well, we tried to do business with a former player. We tried to do business with a minority, but he didn't come through. We gave him every opportunity."

I think, in reality, it was a token gesture by the NFL, but we didn't look at it that way. We said, "We might be a token, but we consider ourselves pioneers. We decided we were going to make this work. We were going to be a success story so that when the next African-American came to the NFL to do business, they wouldn't be able to tell him that O.J. Simpson story any more. They would be able to say, 'Well, if Drew Pearson could do it, maybe you guys can pull it off as well.'

We got the National Basketball Association license through my efforts with David Stern. I wrote him a letter complimenting him on the progressive things he had done for the NBA in the area of involving minorities on the coaching level and in management. I told him that one thing the NBA lacked was a track record of doing business with minority companies. I sent the letter to him by FedEx and within the same week we got a call from the NBA asking us to meet with them. We signed a licensing agreement with them and they continue to this day to be one of our most cherished business associates.

It wasn't easy to get in, but once we did, we also established a long lasting relationship with the National Hockey League. Reverend Jackson helped us get this license and he probably doesn't even know it. I sent a letter to Commissioner Gary Bettman to arrange a meeting with him, and I copied the letter to Reverend Jackson. The letter got us a meeting and we went to New York to meet with Bettman and an attorney. Bettman immediately reamed us because we had copied the letter to Reverend Jackson. He asked, "Is he a partner of yours? What is this reference to Reverend Jackson?" Then he asked, "Do you want the business because of Reverend Jackson or do you want the business because you're qualified?" He gave us a hard time but we came out of there with a license.

I learned that you should never say anything about the meeting you've attended until you leave the building. We were walking down the hall after the meeting and I said to Mike, "We got beat up but at least using Reverend Jackson's name got us a meeting."

Someone in the hallway heard my comment and told Bettman. When I got back to Dallas, Bettman phoned and said, "I don't want to hear anything about Reverend Jackson again, and I don't want to see his name copied on any more letters."

After we got the license, I wrote Bettman thanking him and I copied Reverend Jackson. I guess that was bold, but the NHL has remained a great partner over the years.

Other licenses with several colleges, Warner Brothers, NASCAR and wrestling eventually fell into place. NASCAR was receptive. They welcomed opportunities for minorities to do business with them. They have also been a great partner. Through NASCAR, other things developed, including brands that support the race car drivers. We make hats for Valvoline, Chevy, Ford, and many others because of the NASCAR license.

After what we considered to be an excellent nine-year relationship, the NFL ended our licensing agreement. They didn't give us any valid reason. At the time I played for the Cowboys, through the early 70's and 80's, the Cowboys accounted for 56% of all NFL merchandise sold. It was the players that made it happen. Having the NFL cut us out of the game was extremely disappointing.

Drew Pearson Marketing paid the NFL much more than the NFL paid me to play the game. I paid my debt to them, as I like to say, "paid in full and then some." My first year's salary was $14,500, and my last year's was $225,000. I'm proud to say that I'm probably the only player that has ever played in the league that paid them back for every cent they paid me, including the travel expenses.

We had all our eggs in that pro basket, and when the NFL pulled the license out from under us, it was a wake-up call. We wanted to find out why they terminated our license. The only possible reason was the fact that I was involved with the XFL during the time. The NFL said that wasn't the reason, but I don't know what other reason there could have been. Drew Pearson Marketing was a good partner, we made money for the league, we sold, I was a former player, and we were a minority business. We had all of the positives going that the NFL should have been happy to be associated with.

The only excuse the NFL gave us was that they signed an exclusive deal with Reebok and gave them all of the merchandising rights for apparel. What we couldn't understand was that Reebok's strength was with Footlockers, Champs, and other upper end stores. Our strength was the mass market with Wal-Mart, Target and K-Mart. Reebok had never been in the mass market and didn't know how to do business there.

We were so strong in the mass market that Wal-Mart, Target and K-Mart wrote letters to the league on our behalf asking why they terminated our license. They told the league that Drew Pearson

Marketing was their number one headwear licensee. They liked to do business with us because we gave them the best product and the most designs to choose from, as well as offer them programs to support their headwear business. After the NFL terminated us, we had a year to sell off our entire inventory. Wal-Mart was so intent on continuing to do business with us that instead of buying headwear from Reebok in 2001, they bought our entire inventory.

Reebok had no right to dictate an exclusive with the NFL and I doubt that their contract agreement allowed them to because the NFL had kept other companies. The ironic part is that the NBA had the same deal with Reebok, but the NBA kept Drew Pearson Marketing in the game. They called us and told us, "Don't worry. You are valuable to us. We need you in the game." They said, "You guys have done a great job. You've built your business, did everything you said you were going to do, and we have no reason to terminate you." I didn't shoot one free throw or make one lay up for the NBA and they kept us in the game. I threw up before every NFL game I played for eleven years. I sweated and gave everything I had to the NFL on and off the field, and they cut me. Go figure.

Baseball also kept us on board, but it took some doing. In September of 2001 they sent us a letter of termination. We were devastated because after the NFL, baseball was our number one seller.

At the same time baseball sent us a letter of termination, there was all of this talk by Bud Selig, the commissioner, about minorities in business. He even sent memos making it mandatory that they interview a set number of minority applicants for front office and coaching positions when available. His daughter ran the Milwaukee Brewers for him while he was commissioner and there were articles in *USA Today* and the *New York Times* about Bud Selig being pro-minority and all-inclusive. In reality we were the only African American company they were doing business with and they terminated us. I wrote a letter to Bud and pointed this out.

Major League Baseball Properties responded and said they were going to give us our day in court. They gave us a chance to come to New York, meet with the powers that be and make a presentation about why we shouldn't be terminated.

Ken Shead and Mike Russell were bought out, so I went to New York with one of my new partners, Dave Briskie. We made a strong presentation. We met with Bob Dupay, Bud Selig's right hand man; Tim Bronson, Sr. V.P., who was in charge of Major League Baseball licensing; Howard Smith, the man we communicated with for baseball licensing; Steve Armis, account executive who handled Drew Pearson Marketing and an attorney for Major League Baseball. On our side, there was just Dave and me. I started the presentation by talking about my life as a kid, making the Cowboys, life after football and starting the business. I told them, "This is me. If you take this license away from me, you're taking a part of me."

Dave gave them the facts and the numbers. He talked about what we've done for Major League Baseball, what potential orders we already had on the books, and our relationship with the retailers. They didn't make any decision then but acknowledged that we had presented a compelling argument as to why we should stay in the business.

Two weeks later we got another call from baseball asking when we could return to New York. Dave and I flew there again and sat in a conference room with the same people. Their attitude was different. They were more upbeat and friendly and not at all confrontational. They thanked us for coming on short notice and then read us the riot act. They told why they had terminated us, which was covered in the first meeting and we thought we had satisfied them on those issues. Then out of the blue they said, "We're going to keep you in the game. We're going to tear up the termination and bring you back on board. You'll continue as a licensee for Major League Baseball."

We shook hands and left the meeting. Dave and I were standing on Park Avenue and I looked at him and asked, "Did we win here? I'm pretty sore from the whipping we took in there." We were so stunned from being put in our place that it was hard to realize that we got the license back. This was unprecedented. No one got terminated by a pro sports league and then had their license returned.

This took place in September and I had contacted Reverend Jackson who had called Bud Selig on our behalf. I called Richard Lapchick of the Northeastern Society for Fairness in Sports. Richard had seen the discrimination in sport. So, after he grew up, he committed to try to level the playing field. Richard made calls on my behalf, and our retailers sent messages to the commissioner. We were extremely grateful for the support and knew that it was through the efforts of many people that we got the license back. We have been a licensee with Major League Baseball ever since.

It is ironic that other major league sports leagues accommodated us and saw our value, while the league I played for couldn't see that, and didn't understand.

It was important for us to stay connected with pro football and we were able to make a deal with the Arena Football League. We have their sideline rights and the headwear license as well.

We also started a Legends Collection line of NFL Hall of Famers, who were upset with the NFL. The NFL was using their names and likenesses on merchandise and they weren't getting their fair share of the revenue. They wanted a larger share and the league and the Hall of Fame Committee refused to give it to them. As a result, the players formed their own association to do their licensing. They approached us about doing the apparel for what they wanted to call their Legends Collection line. We felt this was a tremendous opportunity and went to work on it. We convinced them that they could earn more money by associating with us and PPI Marketing, a company owned by Roger Staubach, than they could with anyone else.

Roger's company got involved. Since he was a Hall of Famer, Roger was critical in getting the players on board. It was a joint venture where we made all the hats, a company called Coliseum made the jerseys, and Roger's company marketed it.

We made a presentation to Champs Sporting Goods and they were excited about this program. They wanted to carry the Legends Collection exclusively in all their stores. We thought it was perfect but the NFL heard about it and called Roger to get Roger to back out of the deal so the NFL could do it with Reebok. Roger stood his ground, did not waiver and the NFL was disappointed.

After Roger said no, the NFL went to Reebok and Reebok told Champs, "If you sell this product, you're not going to get Reebok jerseys or other Reebok products." That scared Champs and they backed out. They said they didn't want to carry the product.

The NFL then tried to get the players, but the players wouldn't budge. Players felt that the NFL had every opportunity to give them their fair share of revenue. Some of these guys really needed it. We had a board of directors meeting with the Association of Hall of Fame Players, including Nick Buoniconti, Merlin Olsen, Tom Mack, and Ted Hendricks. We made our presentation and told them what we could do in merchandising. These players were in their mid 50's to 60's. They were beat up physically. Olsen got up to get a drink. He grabbed his cane and limped to the table. He propped himself on the table and set the cane down so he could use both hands to pour himself a drink. Then, he took the glass and limped back to his seat. He held the glass in beat-up hands. If he pointed you wouldn't know what direction to go because his hands were bent and his knuckles were swollen. Olsen had given everything to the game. All of these guys had given everything to the game. They were legends; they *were* the game. For them to have to fight the NFL for anything was something I couldn't understand.

Of all the leagues, the NBA does the best job with its former players. You see them on commercials. They treat them well. They want them to be involved with All Star games and the championships. There are more NBA coaches and players in its front office than any other league. Baseball is the same way. They honor their All Stars and all time players. But the NFL doesn't do that. They might promote that Cowboys team of the 70's or the Steel Curtain or the Miami Dolphins undefeated team, but they don't honor guys individually. When you're out of the game with the NFL, you're gone. That's what many of us felt in that meeting. We felt like the league had turned its back on its own.

The players didn't want much. All they wanted was a fair share of the revenue created by merchandise that used their name, likeness or presence. The NFL could have done that; it wasn't that much. Staubach, on behalf of the other partners, stepped up and guaranteed eighty or so NFL players a fair share. We would generate money to help pay the guaranteed fees to these NFL Hall of Famers. If Staubach could do that, why couldn't the NFL? Why couldn't they help their constituency? They would get nothing but positives out of it. It is hard to understand why the NFL doesn't embrace their own and make them a part of things like the other pro sports leagues do.

We kept this Legends Collection line going. We never gave in. The NFL was upset and told us that if we did anything using their marks, logos or colors in association with these players they would sue us. I don't think they could have won the lawsuit, as long as we didn't use the logos. If, for example, we had used a Paul Horning green and gold jersey, how could they have won that case? But the NFL had deep pockets and they could have tied us up for a long time in court. We didn't want to be battling the NFL like that. We decided to do the jerseys in neutral colors and the program has taken off without the NFL's blessing and without the team colors. There was no question that the program could be much more effective with the team logos and the team colors, but it hasn't come yet. We'll keep trying, and hopefully, the NFL will come around.

What we tried to do is build this Legends Collection to where the NFL has to come to us and say, "Hey, let's bring this in-house." They could be making money off of this as well. I think we're on track to do that. It is a way for Drew Pearson Marketing to stay involved with sports. When the Reebok deal eventually runs out, we want to be there ready and qualified to do business with the league.

Drew Pearson Marketing is strong and diversified. We're into other promotions for apparel, jeans, T-shirts and things of that nature. We haven't gone from selling hats to selling cars, or from selling hats to selling sodas, but from selling hats to selling T-shirts, jackets, and jerseys. We stayed in the apparel business where our experience lies. We started in 1985, so in 2005 it will be 20 years in the business. That's not bad for a company that was expected to fail; not bad for a business that was operating in an industry that was extremely competitive.

We went against Nike, Reebok, Adidas, Fila, Puma, Pony and all those companies that were in the business of sports apparel merchandising. We've seen the industry change and many of those companies have gone under or been gobbled up by the big boys. Here we are, a small independent company that nobody expected to survive, and we're well respected and thriving. I used to tell my guys, "We have nothing to be ashamed of because we did it the right way." Nobody gave us anything. We worked for everything we got and we made things happen for ourselves. All we needed were the opportunities to do it and when granted those opportunities, we took advantage of them. Every situation that we got into with the licensors was a situation where they gave us a tiny piece of the business, something to get in the door. From there we expanded our foothold on a gradual basis to where we had exclusives with Disney and Warner Brothers, and exclusives in serving tiers of the market with some of the other licensors. We've established ourselves and it wasn't easy. We should feel no guilt for any success we've attained because we not only worked for it, but we've done it for a long time.

Drew Pearson Marketing does 95% of its headwear manufacturing. There are many reasons why this is a positive. The biggest is to get our production and orders out on time. We deliver like we say we're going to deliver, but we also get the quality and pricing as well. When Mike Russell and Ken Shead decided to move on, Pauline Ngan, who owns factories in China, bought their interests. She had made our hats and kept a close eye on our company. She wanted to get involved in the business a little more. This was a major coup for Drew Pearson Marketing because of her financial strength, business expertise and the fact that she owns the factories that make our products.

Nike and Adidas are huge companies. Being associated with a factory that makes the same product for them would have caused our product to get pushed back, delaying our delivery times and dates. We became the number one customer for Mainland Sewing, the factories that make our headwear.

I've visited the facilities in China. We've heard a lot about sweat shops and low wages, and although the labor costs are much cheaper than in the States, the Mainland Sewing factories are beautiful facilities. While you're driving there, you pass people riding bikes and walking. They are pulling rickshaws with wood, baskets, furniture, food, plants and other items of necessity. You look at people on the streets and see how impoverished they are. The jobs in the factories are top of the line employment. I'm not saying that every factory overseas is like that, but I know that Mainland Sewing and the factories that Drew Pearson Marketing are associated with are like that. They are air-conditioned and people are treated well. People are in line trying to get those jobs.

Getting involved with Pauline was what we needed to take our company to next level.

CHAPTER TWENTY-SEVEN
★★★★★

Because Drew Pearson Marketing was a licensee with the World Wrestling Federation a relationship was formed that allowed me to get involved with Vince McMahan and the creation of the XFL. Initially, my only interest was becoming a headwear licensee with the new football league. After we got that in place, however, they asked me to be on the advisory board of the XFL.

To be asked to be part of this new league was big for me. Being on the advisory committee, I was instrumental in offering them suggestions on how games should be played. From day one, I told them, "You can call yourself a pro football league, but you're not going to be pro football caliber from day one. It's going to take time to develop credibility." They were more interested in marketing the league, selling tickets and promoting. That was good; they needed that. But, I was more concerned about the game, because to me, the game was the product. You could attract fans because it was new and exciting and the WWF was involved. However, the goal should have been to keep them coming back. The first night, our ratings were high, but they kept going down every week. Eventually, we were the lowest rated program ever shown on prime time TV. This was simply because the product wasn't good. You cannot build a pro football league in eight months and expect it to be a credible product on the field.

We only had six weeks to put the teams together. I was concerned about that. Through that advisory position, I kept trying to stress the product. They wanted to talk marketing and promotion; I wanted to talk product. They wanted to talk rules; I talked product. Taking the time to develop the players and the league was important. In a situation like that, you only have one shot, so you want it to be your best shot.

As a result of my vocal positions on the advisory board, they asked if I would be interested in a general manager's position with one of the teams, especially if they got a deal done in Dallas. After the Dallas team did not materialize, they asked if I would take over the New York team. I was interested in the New York offer because it would be like going back home. It was in close proximity to Jersey and my family.

The XFL worked out a deal to pay one million dollars in rent to play in Giants Stadium. The New York team was the most important team to the new league because of the potentially big market.

When we started negotiating a contract and they made their first offer, I said, "No, that's not enough for me to give up what I have and move from Dallas to New Jersey." I would have to leave my business and put it in someone else's hands. I told them I'd rather stay on the advisory board. It wasn't a negotiating ploy because I had a set figure in my head that it would take for me to accept the job. Even at that, I knew I would be taking a risk that I would piss off the NFL. Through the whole process, Vince McMahan took pot shots at the NFL. The

NFL didn't give the league any blessings or anything like that. If I was going to jeopardize my relationship with the NFL, I needed to be compensated well.

The XFL finally accepted my figure and I signed a three-year contract. I can say without a doubt, without even knowing what the other general managers were making, that I was the highest paid general manager in that league.

We had a press conference in Giants Stadium at the Stadium Club. I rented limousines to take my family there. My mom was there, as well as my sisters and brothers, and everyone was excited. Vince McMahan introduced me as the vice president/general manager of the New York/New Jersey team. We didn't have a nickname yet.

I was back east with my family and making rounds down the New Jersey Turnpike. I never thought that I would return to Jersey to work or to do anything other than visit family or make appearances. I never saw myself going back there to live. This was a great opportunity so I made the transition. I talked to my business partners and they were all for it because it brought more exposure to the name Drew Pearson. The name was a brand, so any exposure to the name was positive for our business. They were excited about that and they blessed the move.

After I got the job, I traveled back and forth. I was the co-host of The Dallas Cowboys Weekly, on Fox Sports Net, and we taped the show on Wednesday. I was broadcasting the Dallas Cowboys post game show on Sunday. I was in New Jersey from Monday to Wednesday, then I would catch a plane back to Dallas in time to tape my show. I stayed in Dallas and worked the XFL business and Drew Pearson Marketing business. Then, I did the post game show and headed back to Jersey early Monday morning.

I developed my staff and hired everyone from the marketing

guy to the vice president of administration and the secretary. I went through the whole process. I had to look for office space. We worked out deals with the Giants as far as times to practice, what facilities we could use at their practice field, and where our alternative site would be. We worked out deals with high schools and local colleges to use their facilities.

There was much work to be done. We were building a league from the ground up. We didn't have shoulder pads, jock straps, socks, shoes, or anything. We didn't even have a locker room. All of these things caught the league by surprise. I don't think they realized how expensive it would be to build this project.

The entire league worked together because there were only eight general managers. This was different for me because I was accustomed to being the boss. Now I was general manager of a team but since the league owned the teams I had bosses in the league office. I was here, the bosses were there, and I had to answer to them. I had difficulty adjusting to that and was guilty of making decisions on my own without consulting them.

One of the things I had to do after getting the staff in place was to find a head coach. They tried to force feed me some names, but I said, "I think the guy we should make the effort to hire is Charlie Waters."

They were ecstatic. They said, "Yeah, that would be great for New York. Let's try to get him."

I approached Charlie over lunch at S&D Oyster Bar on McKinney Avenue and Charlie was interested. However, after several days of deliberation, he graciously turned me down.

When Charlie turned me down, my attention turned to Danny White. Danny was coaching the Arizona Rattlers in the Arena Football

League and won championships there. I knew Danny and figured what kind of offense he would put in. It would be Landry's kind of offense. I knew he was a leader. After eight or nine years in the Arena Football League, I figured he might be looking for an opportunity to show his coaching talents on the big field as opposed to the 50-yard field of the indoor arena.

I made a call to Danny and he was interested, initially. I went to Arizona to visit with him and he continued to show interest in it. After several weeks, however, Danny turned me down. Now I didn't know who to go with.

The league started throwing names at me and one of them was Rusty Tillman. I remembered Rusty from his playing days with the Redskins. He was the Kamikaze guy who busted the wedge. He made a career on special teams with the Redskins. He was then the special teams coach with Seattle.

The league arranged for a meeting with Rusty during an XFL tryout at the University of North Texas. As the players worked out, Rusty and I sat in the stands and talked for a couple of hours. We discussed his philosophies of offense, defense and special teams.

The more I talked to him, the more fired up he got. His face turned red. Tillman talked about the commitment he would make and how he wanted the job.

I talked to the owners about Rusty and said, "I think we can make this work, even though he's a Redskin. We can mix the Redskin with the Cowboy and make it good for the NewYork/New Jersey team." I thought about it for another day, and that Monday I called Rusty.

Rusty's wife answered the phone. She said, "Hold on, hold on. I'll get him for you."

He came to the phone and I messed with him at first. I said,

"Well, I don't know Rusty. You're a Redskin, and I just don't think it's gonna work . . . unless, you tell me it can work."

He said, "It'll work, it'll work. I'll make it work."

I told him, "Then you're my coach."

He said, "Oh, man!" He was yelling. You could hear his wife and kids yelling in the background. He told me, "Thank you, thank you, thank you so much. You won't regret this decision. Trust me." I found out later that his favorite saying was "Trust me." From then on, everything was "Trust me." When I called him into the office after we had lost our first three games, he said, "Trust me Drew. I'm going to turn this thing around. Just trust me."

We had a press conference to introduce Rusty at the WWF Club in Manhattan, on Times Square. The room was packed. I introduced Rusty. He talked to the reporters and got red faced and fired up. It turned out later that our colors were black and blue. He even wore a black suit with a blue shirt. Rusty was intense and he coached that way.

We had a draft in November and the next week, we had a mini camp and brought in all the specialty players. The first week in December, we had another mini camp where we brought in all the players. Then, three weeks later, we opened training camp. That was in January. Four teams trained in Las Vegas, and four trained in Orlando, Florida. We went to Orlando. That allowed the teams to practice against each other.

We practiced at a high school field and stayed at a Radisson Hotel. Four weeks were not enough. I could see it. We weren't close to being a team, let alone a pro team. We did not have a chance to draft players, sign free agents, and then say, "Well, he wasn't good enough." If he wasn't good enough or was a bad pick, we had to keep him on the team and make something out of him.

Halfway through the four weeks, Vince McMahan, Dick Ebersole and Ken Shantzer from NBC Sports brought in four of the teams to talk about the XFL. This was January and the first game was scheduled for February 10. Vince got up and started talking and rah-rahing. He said, "Screw the NFL. We're going to show them. There's an alternative in pro football. We're gonna do it exciting and we're gonna have fun." He wasn't saying anything about the teams.

Then Ebersole got up and said, "Here is what NBC is going to do. We're gonna have the commercials. We're gonna hype this and promote it all through the NFL football season. And instead of talking about the NFL, we're going to talk XFL. We're going to have you on prime time Saturday nights." Ebersole was upset because this was the first time NBC didn't have NFL football. Their purpose of getting involved with the XFL was to have professional football.

We had our first dry-run scrimmage the next week. That was the first time I saw XFL competition. I don't think Vince was there, the NBC people were only there to test their equipment. They had no concerns about the quality of the game. I watched the first scrimmage and it was competitive only because both teams were sorry. No one had developed a team yet. We had two weeks to get this together, but it didn't happen.

We left New Jersey for our first game in Las Vegas on Saturday night and if anything could go wrong, it did. I planned for us to arrive, have a pre-game meal, a meeting, and curfew. We would get up and play the game that night and leave town. I wanted to keep the schedule as tight as possible to avoid thinking about the time change. From Jersey to Las Vegas is three hours, so there is a big time adjustment.

This was the first game of the season, and it was on national

TV. The league called me to say that they were going to charter a flight for us on Thursday. There was only one problem with that. The charter left from JFK Airport in New York City. Kennedy was only fifteen miles away, but it took us three hours to go that fifteen miles. We were stuck in a traffic jam on one of the bridges and Rusty nearly got all of us thrown in jail because he got out of the bus and started raising hell with a cop.

With all of the great hotels in Vegas, they had us staying at the Palace Station. I'd never heard of this place, and for good reason. We walked into the lobby and got hit with a wall of cigarette smoke. Guys started coughing. I said, "Oh, well. Maybe the rooms aren't that bad." You figure that in Vegas everyone smokes anyway. We got the players to their rooms, but the next thing we knew, they were all coming back down.

I asked. "What's wrong?"

They said, "Coach, these are all smoking rooms. We can't even sleep in these rooms."

I went to the front desk and asked if they had any non-smoking rooms. They said, "No."

I said, "Hey guys, this is the XFL. You'll have to make the best of it. Go down to the store and get something to spray your room."

The next issue was practice. They changed our practice time four or five times. We said, "To hell with them. We're going to go practice at the time we are scheduled."

We arrived to practice as the other XFL team was leaving the field. Half way through practice, the sprinklers came on. I think it happened on purpose. By the time the sprinklers were turned off, we were soaking wet. We said, "To hell with it!" And called off practice.

When we got back to the hotel to prepare for the game, the

place was buzzing. My phone didn't stop ringing. People called from all over the country. They were saying, "Good luck, Drew. We'll be watching."

I knew we weren't quality. I watched all the commercials on NBC hyping the XFL. They had land mines blowing up and all of this artillery promoting the XFL. They never showed one football player. If I did one interview that Saturday, I did a hundred. I did them in California, New York, Dallas, and all over the country. Everyone called wanting interviews because they were hyped for the XFL.

There was tailgating everywhere and the stadium was packed. I noticed that it was a different kind of fan. They were not typical football fans. They were more like typical wrestling fans. They were more concerned with seeing Vince McMahan and The Rock, than the football teams. Once they started drinking, it got scary. They didn't know me and were yelling, "Pearson, you suck! You couldn't play no ball. The Cowboys suck!"

They had a seat for me in the press box, but I couldn't stay there. I had to be on the sidelines. I stood on the sidelines for the game and we stunk up the joint. We played terrible. We played hard and aggressive, but we had no execution or continuity. We had a 19-0 blowout loss in our first game on NBC. My phone didn't ring after that. No one called. I hoped someone would because I needed condolences and sympathy.

I was totally embarrassed, not so much by my team's performance, but by the fact that the league let it happen. My plan would have been to spend an entire year to develop and promote the XFL. Every month within that year, I would have announced a new team. That would have created a new market, new team, new colors and new nickname. We would also have had a year to develop the teams. We should have had those players practicing for a year before they played.

I think the thing that killed the league was NBC's involvement. Vince McMahan and Basil DiVito had a great business plan for the XFL. The problem was that they wavered from that plan when NBC got involved. NBC put a lot of money into it and made it an equal partnership. The network wanted something instantly. They wanted to fill that football void in their programming. They forced the issue as far as getting it out there, hyping it and making it bigger than it would ever be.

The first year was a disaster as far as NBC's ratings were concerned, but we were also on UPN and TNN and they were excited with the ratings. UPN and TNN wanted to continue into the second year but NBC didn't. Having two outlets televising games for a start-up league would have been great, but UPN was holding the XFL's feet to the fire because they wanted a better deal with the WWF. The WWF was the number one program on UPN at that time, and UPN wanted to take away something from the deal with the XFL.

Vince looked at the money that was lost in the first year, and at what the WWF was doing. The people on his board of directors didn't want to mess with their crown jewel. They went through some serious negotiations until UPN was ready to televise two games per week. TNN was also going to televise a game, so there would have been three games a week on TV. But they said "No" when UPN wanted to renegotiate the WWF contract, so the TV deal with them fell through and that was when the league decided to fold.

At seasons end, I went to Stanford, Connecticut where the WWF and the XFL headquarters were housed. All the general managers were there. We met for two days discussing the first season and the upcoming season. We talked about what direction we were going and what we were going to do to cut costs. Vince addressed us. He said, "Everything's good. We lost a lot of money, but we're committed to this thing and we're going to try to make it work. We'll do everything we can to keep it going." He told us that it looked like NBC wouldn't be a partner in the second round, but there were still possibilities with UPN and TNN.

We came out of there fired up and went back to our offices thinking that we were going to have another season. An order of new furniture worth $70,000 was coming in from Florida. After using makeshift furniture during the first season, I thought, *If they were going to fold after the first year, they would have cancelled this order.*

We were on the 10th floor of a high-rise office building. I could look out of my office window and see Giants Stadium and the skyline of New York City. This was great. The furniture, classy stuff, and our offices took on a new look. We even had special computers for the coaches. They were making a commitment, and after I came out of the meeting for the general managers, I figured we were definitely going to be around for another year.

I was invited by the New Jersey Exposition Authority, which owns Giants Stadium, to a press conference commemorating their 25th anniversary. They also invited people from the Giants and the Jets, and anyone who did business with Giants Stadium. After we were introduced, all of the reporters approached me. Their biggest concern was whether the XFL would survive. I said, "Oh, yeah! We just had a meeting with the general managers and Vince McMahan says that there is no question that we're going into the second year. As a matter of fact, the coaches are in Stanford, Connecticut, this week meeting. I got a call from Rusty and he says everything is going great. Vince has assured them that we'll be here another year."

I got back to the office and worked a couple of hours. Rusty called as he was getting ready to cross the George Washington Bridge. Traffic was backed up because someone was getting ready to jump off the bridge. Rusty told me about the meetings, "We had a great meeting and Vince got us all pumped up. All of the coaches are fired up"

As I hung up, I told Rusty, "You be safe, and I'll see you when you get to the office."

An hour later, I got a call from the league saying, "Drew, we're going to have a conference call with the general managers at 5:45 and then at 6:00 we're going to have a conference call with all of the employees."

I brought in Paul Miles, V.P. of Administration and Richard Oriolo, my vice president of marketing. We were in my office and wondering what it was all about. We talked about everything, cutting expenses or something along those lines, because nobody thought about folding. We had just gotten furniture. We had a million dollar deal on the table with Giants Stadium. We had commitments with colleges, hotels, car people, apartment people, equipment people, and leases for office equipment. Nobody was thinking that this was going to end. We thought maybe it was going to be a pep talk.

The time for the call arrived and the first thing they told us was, "Make sure no one is in your office."

When the call came I had everyone in the office and had told them to be quiet. They heard the announcement. I was in shock. Basil spoke and you could tell something was wrong by the tone of his voice. He said, "I don't know how to tell you this other than to just tell you. We're folding the league and we're stopping operations immediately." Then Vince said something and the next thing you know everyone was upset. The secretary started sobbing. I tried to quiet them because they weren't supposed to be listening. They had to leave the room. The call lasted five minutes. There were no questions taken and no reason given as to why this was happening.

They came with the 6:00 p.m. conference call, which was also short. My staff knew about it and they were all crying. Many people had made tremendous sacrifices. My public relations man was getting married in two weeks. He had made a commitment on a house. Another employee had just signed a lease on a new apartment. Someone else was bringing his family from Florida and was making all of the adjustments for school. People made these sacrifices, and all of a sudden, the league was gone.

I was mad! I was upset because we had established some credibility. Even though the quality of our games wasn't the greatest, the quality improved every week as the season continued. By the end of the season, our games were competitive. We had at least seven NFL scouts at our games. I got calls saying, "Drew, I need a press pass. We're going to be at the game scouting certain players." We still had TV contracts. We had relationships with the stadiums and facilities to play in.

If I thought my business was going to fail, I would sell whatever I could before I shut it down. I'd sell the whole damn league. I got word that the NFL was interested. There were probably investors who were interested in investing in the teams in different markets instead of the league owning all the teams. They could have gotten investors to buy these teams. They could have raised money and saved the league some way. But, they just cut their losses right there, and did it in a brutal way. From then on, it was crisis management in the office and in dealing with people.

The league was concerned about transitioning out of the things that it was involved in and I was more concerned about transitioning myself out. I had made a tremendous commitment to this league. I had uprooted myself and was away from my family, business, and business partners.

When the league folded I stayed a short time through the transition. But because of the negatives associated with the way they shut it down, I told them that I didn't want to be part of it. I was done from there.

I have no regrets with the XFL. I'm glad I tried it. The only regret I have is that we couldn't make it work.

CHAPTER TWENTY-EIGHT
★★★★★

My life has been filled with blessings and I thank God every day for these blessings. I lived the American Dream because of a little bit of athletic ability, hard work, and a desire not to disappoint my family and friends. When you get in trouble or fail to do your best it reflects on your family. They're the ones bragging about you, talking about you, and walking around with their chests out because of what you've accomplished. They're proud of you, so when you do something bad, it affects not only your immediate family, but down the line as well. As a role model for my kids and family, I try to do the right things. If other people want to emulate me that's fine, because I feel I have a responsibility to them, too. If somebody admires you for what you do, you have a responsibility because you're providing motivation and inspiration to them. That's how it's all connected. If you don't do the right things and get in trouble you let down your immediate family, extended family, friends and fans. How many of them are out there? It's a big responsibility to do the right things and make sure you don't embarrass your immediate family. If you don't let them down, you won't let anyone down. Then, maybe you will be someone others want to pattern their lives after who will give others the motivation to succeed and reach the levels of success that they're capable of.

I believe that it is the responsibility of every adult to be a positive example for our children. The most important role models for our youth shouldn't be athletes. Society admires us because of the exposure we get. In reality, we are a three-hour football game, a two-hour basketball game, a nine-inning baseball game, or a 60-second commercial in kids' lives. The true role models should be the people who are affecting kids on a daily basis, like their parents, teachers, counselors or pastors.

I've always thought teachers should be our highest paid professionals because of their enormous responsibilities. Teachers should be getting the big bucks. We should inspire more people with the ability to become teachers. There are many who have the talent to teach but do not go into the teaching profession because of the low pay scales. The influence that they have over kids should be much greater than sports figures. Teaching is the most slighted profession in our working system. We take teachers for granted.

I've had the opportunity to speak at educational functions. I tell the teachers, counselors, and administrators in the audience that they are my role models. When I was growing up, teachers gave me the greatest inspiration to achieve. The best was Ms. Gracie Dunn, my 10th grade English Literature teacher. I had trouble with Shakespearian literature. I was a black guy from South River and had never encountered this type of language before. It was difficult to grasp. Ms. Dunn must have believed I could learn because she stayed on me constantly.

Every time I opened that book and read Shakespearian literature, I tried a little harder because I wanted to pass, graduate from high school, and go to college. I passed her class, with a C average in English throughout high school, and had a B average in English in college. After I went back to Tulsa and finished my degree, I wanted to go home and show Ms. Dunn what I had done. I wanted to tell her how she had provided the inspiration. Unfortunately, she had passed away. To this day, even at age 53, I think about Ms. Gracie Dunn.

That is how teachers influence people. If you send your kids off and give them to someone for six or eight hours a day, you should have confidence that you are putting them in the best available hands. Hopefully, in due time, the situation will change and teachers will be given the respect they deserve. If you have an education, you have a better chance to succeed. I believe that our educational system is the only institution that makes the American Dream possible for everyone.

I have received many awards for my football accomplishments. They were all greatly appreciated but the best awards, the ones that mean most to me, are the ones related to education. There are three that come to mind. I was selected for an honorary Doctor of Law degree at Wiley College in Marshall, Texas. It was humbling to be considered for something like that, let alone to receive it. I received a distinguished alumni award from the University of Tulsa. I also received a Silver Anniversary Award from the NCAA. It was an award given to a student athlete 25 years after graduating from college for significant accomplishments achieved during that time. Those awards are linked to the positive relationships I have developed and my accomplishments related to the education I received.

COWBOYS

CHAPTER TWENTY-NINE
★★★★★

Harvey Martin was my best friend. We hung out together and got to know each other well because our names, beginning with M and P, fell after one another in the alphabet. We were roommates in training camp, after we broke training camp, and on the road after we had made the Cowboys team.

Harvey was born in Dallas, so he knew all about the city. He knew how to get around; he knew all of the right people, and the best restaurants to go to. I tagged along with Harvey, trying to learn Dallas. He told me about the realities of Dallas before we made the team in 1973. He told me about how racist Dallas once had been with separate drinking fountains, separate rest rooms, and segregated schools. It surprised me because I had no idea that had gone on. I'd heard about it in other places but I'd never expected it in the Dallas I knew.

When we broke camp and got back to Dallas our rookie year, we stayed at the 6060 Hotel on Central Expressway by the Cowboys' office. The first night back, we had an 11:00 p.m. curfew and I went out with Harvey. We went to a club, the Sports Page, where Mike Ditka was part owner. Ditka and Dan Reeves, who was also a Cowboys coach, were there, and we got busted for curfew violations. I was scared. First of all, I was married and I knew my wife was going to be mad. Second, Coach Landry was not going to be happy about rookies being out that late. We got fined $150, which was a week's pay. They took it out of our checks at the end of the week and we got three zero's on our checks. The Cowboys had the nerve to give us the checks anyway. Harvey and I took those checks and stuck them in our playbooks as a reminder not to get busted again.

Harvey was a great guy and a genuine person. The thing I loved about Harvey was that he was so generous. I think that was his downfall later in life. He accepted all people and brought them into his life easily. Many of those people weren't there for the right reasons and Harvey was friendly and gullible. People took advantage of his kindness and that's what got him into trouble. Harvey loved playing football in Dallas and being a Dallas Cowboy. He loved being there because he was close to his mom and family.

As a player, the trait that stands out most about Harvey was his intensity. He would get so fired up for a game that sometimes it was scary. I was a wide receiver. I needed my sleep. I had to run all day to make something happen. Harvey needed his sleep too, but he was too nervous the night before to get much rest. The nights before road games, Harvey talked on the phone and had the TV on. His ritual was to order room service. After we got into town, we had a scheduled meal. Then, before we went to bed, they had a snack for us. After 11:00 p.m. curfew, Harvey would order room service. He didn't know what he wanted, so he ordered four or five different items, including dessert. Everything would come, and I could smell the onions, cheese, and meat while I tried to sleep. Whatever he ordered smelled all night. I tried to sleep with a pillow over my head, tossing and turning. The whole time, Harvey talked to me, "Homeboy, I'm gonna kill that guy in front of me, man. I can't wait to get him."

I would say, "Harvey, you've got to get some sleep first before you do anything." He was so intense that on game day, even though he hadn't had much sleep, he'd be up early and ready to go. He never ate any breakfast because he had been eating all night. We always went to the game early in a cab, ahead of the team. When we got to the stadium, the first thing we smelled was the stadium hot dogs. That aroma would be so good. Harvey would look at me and I would look at him and we would say, "Yeah, we've gotta have one."

When we got to the locker room the first thing we did was send the ball boy upstairs to get hot dogs. Harvey ate about four and I tried to eat one. I knew I didn't need to eat because I had a nervous stomach before every game. Harvey would tear them up. That would be his pre-game meal — hot dogs with mustard and relish.

Life after football was tough for Harvey. He tried to make the adjustment but had too many people coming at him. He got sidetracked, but the things I know about Harvey Martin are all good. When he passed away it was a sad day. Harvey had so much pride that he didn't want anybody to know that he was sick. That's why, as his best friend, I didn't know. I didn't know until it was near the point of no return for Harvey. He didn't want anybody to see him like that. Robert Newhouse called me and told me that Harvey was sick in the hospital and that I needed to go see him. I was shocked because I didn't know Harvey's cancer had progressed that far.

The first time I went to see him I couldn't go alone. I called Jay Saldi and we went together. When we first saw Harvey, we started crying because he didn't look like Harvey. He was still big, but there wasn't much tissue on his bones. The first thing he said when we walked into the room was, "Aye, Dawg!" He used to call me "Dawg" all the time.

It was tough to see him like that. I was with him in his final days along with his mother, daughter, and son. I was there when the doctor told him that it wouldn't be much longer. I think that was the first time Harvey knew he wasn't going to make it. He was shocked. The doctors asked him, "If certain things stop, do you want us to keep fighting?"

Harvey said, "Hell yes!"

After the doctor left, I went outside and I said, "Doc, It looks to me like Harvey is improving. He looks like he's getting better. He wants to get up and he's eating more."

The doctor said, "Drew, what you don't see is that he is dying inside. His organs are shutting down."

I went back into the room and Harvey's eyes were wide open. He was wide-awake and wanted to know what was going on. He asked what the doctor had said. I told him, "They don't think you're going to make it." You could see the tears coming out of his eyes and I said, " Harvey, he's a doctor, he ain't God. That means you're in God's hands now. You've got to feel comfort in that."

There was a daily calendar on the wall. When the nurses came in every day, they pulled a number off that calendar. I said, "Harvey, what you want to do is see that number change every day." From that time until he passed away a few days later, Harvey fixed his eyes on that calendar. He lay in bed looking at the calendar, waiting for it to change. I'm glad to know that before he did pass, he was at peace with himself. He had come to grips with the situation.

It was just like Harvey to never complain. He never said, "Why me?" He never said, "Look at you Drew. You're healthy. How come you're not here and I am?" He was never that way. So from there it was a matter of comforting his family, especially his mother.

Harvey used to get on me all of the time saying, "You need to call your mother."

I'd say, "Yeah, I'm going to call her."

"You need to call her right now. You don't need a reason to call her," he'd say, "just call her." That's how close he was with his mother.

He was one great football player. There's no question he is Ring of Honor and Hall of Fame material. Even though he passed on, hopefully someday in the near future he'll finally get the recognition he deserves. It would be such a tribute for his mother to accept these honors on his behalf.

I guess that it's obvious I am very passionate about my relationship with Harvey and emotional about his passing. We were the same age. When Too Tall, Billy Joe, Newhouse, and I do autograph sessions together and there's no Harvey, it's as though a huge void has been created. But one thing we all learned from Harvey was how to handle something tough. If fatal illness ever happens to us, I think we'll handle it better because of Harvey.

He was the one I confided in and the one I got in trouble with. We played together for 11 years. Neither of us ever missed a game. In the training room and on the field, we were warriors. Coach Landry and our teammates knew they could count on us week in and week out.

It was ironic how Harvey, **Billy Joe Dupree**, and I came in at the same time in 1973, played 11 years together and retired during the same off-season, all for different reasons. Harvey retired because he felt the pressure as a result of his issues with drugs. He got tired of it and walked away from the game. There was no question that he could still have played. Billy Joe retired because he wanted to. That's just Billy Joe. It was his time and he wanted to go out on top. There was no question that he could also have played longer. Of course, I retired because of my car accident in 1984. We called ourselves the "decade plus one boys." They were my two closest friends on the team.

Billy Joe was a character. He was so different from us. We used to call him "The Governor," because he was interested in politics and read the *Wall Street Journal*. Sometimes he came into meetings wearing a tie. I'd say, "Billy Joe, where are you going?"

He'd tease, "I've got to go somewhere after this meeting, take care of some business."

I'd say, "Make sure you're back in time because we're only playing the Redskins this week. It might be an important game."

I liked to call Billy Joe eccentric. Even his car was different. He had a Volkswagen, but it wasn't just a Volkswagen. He had the nose done so it looked like a Rolls Royce and the back end was jacked up. Football was always secondary to him. He saw it as an opportunity and a means to something else. He only played football in high school and college because it led to other opportunities that he wanted to explore. He was interested in construction and engineering, and concerned about politics.

Billy Joe was playing golf before golf became popular, especially for African-Americans. Once he took me out to the driving range during our off day. We hit a bucket or two of balls and I looked at my hands. They were covered with blisters and I was upset. I'd never gotten blisters playing football, and I felt stupid getting them by hitting golf balls. My hands were my livelihood and that was pretty much the end of my golf career.

Billy Joe was a great guy. He was a starter from day one in the league, and a starter when he left. Everyone remembers the great catches he made as tight end, but his real strength was blocking. All our running backs, Calvin Hill, Preston Pearson, Doug Dennison and Tony Dorsett, gained most of their yardage running off of Billy Joe. Usually when they ran 36 or 37 Switch, he blocked down on the defensive end, defensive tackle or linebacker, and caved in that side. If you put Billy Joe and Rayfield Wright on the same side, most of the time it was going to be five yards before the running back got touched. When we needed that kind of yardage, Coach Landry ran right over Billy Joe and Rayfield. He didn't get enough recognition or attention as a blocker.

Billy Joe was also a mumbler. He was a big guy, but so soft-spoken that when he talked, you had to move close to hear what he said. Sometimes you failed to understand him. When you did hear what he said it was usually intelligent because he was somewhat of a philosopher. He was the guy that kind of grounded Harvey and me. He was like our anchor. While Harvey and I were doing our thing – we were a lot looser than Billy Joe – Billy Joe was always "Mr. Straight." He came into the league married and he's married to the same woman to this day. He is a special friend.

I had a special bond with **Roger Staubach** that grew from our working relationship. When I came in as a rookie he liked my work ethic and ability to run routes. He went to bat for me with the Cowboys and helped me get $500 so I could quit a job with the moving company and concentrate on making the team.

Roger was a great athlete. He was a self-made athlete, not a natural athlete. He couldn't jump high or run fast. Even though he was called "Roger the Dodger" for elusive moves on the field, he wasn't that mobile or elusive. He made himself special through hard work, knowledge and preparation for the game, and through an attitude that was unbelievable. I guess most people think that stemmed from his Navy background, but I'm willing to say that it probably began a long time before that. It was something he developed as a kid — a tough attitude. Even though Roger was the nicest guy on the team and a morally sound person, he was the last guy you wanted to pick a fight with.

Coach would tell Roger, "Slide, slide. Quit taking that hit." Roger never listened and when a situation arose where we needed that extra yard, he never slid. He stuck his head in there to get that yard. His competitive nature took over. That's how he got knocked out in 1974 against the Redskins when they predicted they were going to knock him out. He tried to fight for the extra yard. He never complained about his injuries; in fact, he never complained about anything.

When Roger retired, it was very difficult for me. I was disappointed but didn't put pressure on him to stay. I wanted him to make his own decision, and his decision wasn't based on his ability to continue to play. He still had the ability and he could have continued to play effectively for several more years. Medical concerns were the only reason he retired. There was a fear that an accumulation of concussions he had suffered might cause problems down the road.

He had to make the decision, and didn't need anyone trying to influence him because of their own selfishness. If the decision was only football, an ability issue, I would have been all over him. I would have cooked him breakfast, washed his car everyday and done anything to keep him in the game for one more year. But since it was medical, I backed off. Besides the concussions, I think the fact that Danny White was ready to step in as a starting quarterback was a factor in Roger's decision. Also, I believe Roger would have stayed if Coach Landry had given him more say in calling plays, not necessarily allowing him to call all the plays but just having more input.

I didn't go to his retirement celebration because I didn't want to be seen crying in public. I watched it on TV. His last words were, "I'm retired." And that made it official. When you play eight years with one quarterback, a quarterback like Staubach, and had been his go-to guy, it was disappointing. I was worried that with him gone my production might go down and that I might be next out the door. At the same time, I knew Roger was going to be all right in retirement. In fact, he is more successful in his life after football than he was as the starting quarterback for the Cowboys.

Danny White became the No. 1 quarterback of the Cowboys and I always had a respectful relationship with him. He was somewhat like Roger in demeanor and personality. He had the same drive and motivation to be the best. He was intelligent and had great athletic ability. Actually, Danny was probably a better all-around athlete than Roger because he was a little faster and more mobile, even though he didn't scramble as much as Roger.

Danny was reserved and there was intense pressure on him as he tried to fill Roger's shoes. Danny wanted to do it in a big way, and he wanted it to happen quickly. One of the things he wanted to do was to establish his own go-to guy, the receiver he could count on in the clutch. Therefore, my production went down. I wasn't getting many balls thrown to me. That was OK because we spread it out. Tony Hill was coming into his own, doing great things, and deserved his share of the passes. Tony was capable, but it was disappointing to me. All we did with the offense was take Roger out and put Danny in. Everything else was set. We had the same receivers, running backs, line, philosophy, plays and terminology. All we did was take one piece out and put another piece in. Danny seemed like he tried to do too much in replacing Roger. It didn't come naturally to him. He had the ability and talents to let the take over occur naturally.

If there was one person you could hand pick to replace Staubach, I think it was White. He still doesn't get enough credit for what he did. When he stepped in, he took us to three straight NFC Championship Games. Unfortunately, we lost those games, but it wasn't because of Danny. He took heavy flak because of that but he had the personality to handle it.

Danny's pass was different than Roger's. Roger threw hard. He prided himself in throwing hard. He wanted to zip the ball. That's why, when I was trying out for the Cowboys, I dropped so many passes. Danny had zip on the ball because you've got to have that in the NFL. His passes didn't come in as hard as Roger's. He threw more on anticipation and timing.

In 1980, when Danny took over his first season, we were 12-4 and went to the NFC Championship Game. In the second season, 1981, we were 12-4 again and went to the Championship Game. The third season was a strike year. We were 6-3, but we made it to the Championship playoff.

Danny was an effective quarterback, but during the strike year he went on his own to get things settled. That turned out to be a negative approach on his part because many teammates objected. They thought he was going behind the Union's back to work a deal with Tex Schramm and get the strike settled. The players didn't take kindly to that because that wasn't our strategy. We felt it eventually hurt us in negotiations.

Because of his involvement in the strike, Danny created a wall between himself and many players. This was unfortunate, because the quarterback can't build a wall between himself and his teammates and remain effective.

We eventually got into a situation where it was either Danny White or Gary Hogeboom. Most of the players were pro Hogeboom because of the position Danny took during the strike. Eventually Coach Landry replaced him, but this was after I was gone.

Bob Hayes was a good friend, and had taken a liking to me during training camp my rookie year. We developed a friendship in the short time we spent together with the Cowboys. The Cowboys traded Bob to San Francisco in 1974. Beyond that, we remained friends after he retired and we often hung out together. It was disappointing when Bob got arrested for his involvement with drugs. After talking with Bob and understanding the situation, I knew the problem. It was the same fault as Harvey's. Hayes was the nicest guy you want to meet. He had a great personality and loved to be around people. He was so friendly that he took in anybody as long as they showed they liked him. It was the same with Harvey. Unfortunately, Bob associated with the wrong people and they took advantage of him. I think it was a case of Hayes being in the wrong place at the wrong time. When his trial came up, I went to court to vouch for him as a character witness. I was there for him throughout the trial but there wasn't much I could do. It hurt to see one of my heroes have to go through that.

Bob had rough times. I tried to be there for him as a friend, and I was. He had other friends that he could count on, especially Staubach. Roger was there for Bob in his tough times and tried to get him back on the right road.

After my rookie season, I was given a testimonial dinner and parade in South River. They asked if I could get a Cowboys player as the guest speaker.

I didn't know who to ask. I thought of Roger, but our friendship was mostly on the field. My friendship with Bob extended beyond the field. We went to dinner, I went to his house for parties, and I knew his wife. His wife at the time, Altamese, was from New Brunswick, New Jersey, next to South River. We used to play them in high school football every Thanksgiving.

I asked Bob and he said he would do it. The banquet was for me, but Bob Hayes in South River, New Jersey, at the Knights of Columbus Hall, created a buzz in town. He was great and stayed the weekend. In fact, he loved it so much, we had to make him leave. The people loved him. He was warm, cordial, and made a nice speech about our relationship. This was the first time I heard him talk about what I meant to him. Having *my* idol talk about *me* was a gratifying experience.

After Bob hit tough times, I met him at a Cowboys game before Christmas. He told me he was staying at a Motel 6.

I told him, "You've gotta get out of there. You come stay with me."

The place where I lived had a garage apartment with a separate entrance, and Bob stayed there for three or four months.

After that, he started to get himself together and moved out on his own. Bob was not just a track athlete that happened to play football. He knew football and was a football player first. He knew how to run pass routes and he knew defenses. He knew how to have his body ready to play every week and go through practices. He was proud of his football record. He was great high school football player in Florida and then at Florida A& M.

Hayes accomplished some amazing things. I had 48 touchdowns in the 11 regular seasons I played, and in the nine years Bob played, he scored 71 touchdowns. Nobody could stop Hayes. Because of him, rivals developed zone defenses. The zone was a containing defense designed mainly to slow Hayes. There were other fast receivers in the league, notably Homer Jones with the New York Giants, but he wasn't burning defenses like Hayes. After two years in the league, he scored 25 touchdowns. This was a bigger splash than Randy Moss, Jerry Rice or Drew Pearson ever made in the NFL. Defenses had to come up with a way to contain him. The zone defense was the way. That slowed his production, but when you note that he averaged 20 yards a catch, it was a phenomenal career. Lay on top of that two gold medals for the U.S. in the Olympics and you wonder, *Why isn't this guy in the NFL Hall of Fame? Why did it take him so long to get in the Cowboy Ring of Honor?*

When Bob died it brought a lot of attention to his accomplishments. People now talk about Bob as a Hall of Famer. Before he died, nobody talked about Bob deserving that type of recognition. Now they see his records. They see his accomplishments. They hear about how he changed defenses. They hear confessions from defensive coordinators on how much of a nightmare it was to prepare for him.

This past year he got close to the Hall of Fame. Three Cowboys were in the final 10 and two in the final six for induction. Four players made it, but no Cowboys. I thought that Bob was going to get in this time and I was disappointed that he didn't. Hopefully one day he'll get that recognition. He won Super Bowls and played in playoff games. He wasn't merely a great player on a bad team; he was a great player on a great team in a great organization. He was a big part of that organization going from a bad team to starting a record of 20 consecutive winning seasons.

Ed "Too Tall" Jones was a tremendous teammate. He was a "gamer". He probably used less equipment than any player on the team. Ed put on shoulder pads, pants, socks and shoes and he was ready for practice. He never taped his hands or ankles. I never saw another player in the NFL without his ankles taped. It was a ritual. First of all, if you sprained an ankle and it wasn't taped, it was a major fine. If you missed a game, then it was going to cost you a game check. So it was prudent for everyone to get his ankles taped. If you didn't want to wait in line for the trainer, you learned to do it yourself. Ed never got his ankles taped. He played 15 years and never missed a game.

There was a big buzz when he came into the league in 1974 as a No. 1 draft pick from Tennessee State. We needed that shot and he became an excellent complement to Harvey Martin. They played the bookends as defensive ends. Ed was nice, quiet, and sort of shy but, when he spoke, people listened because he didn't engage in idle talk. When he did say something it had meaning.

I drove to Jersey every other year when I was on the team and never let my family drive with me. I flew them to meet me because I liked to be alone and that was my time. I drove through Pennsylvania after Ed's fifth year, listening to a radio station from Philadelphia. They started talking about Too Tall Jones retiring from the Cowboys to box. I was stunned. I couldn't believe what I heard. He'd just gotten established in the league and now he was going to boxing? Back then I didn't have cell phone, so I couldn't make a call to verify the story until I got to where I was going. I got to Jersey and the first thing I asked was, "Is it true? Is Too Tall going into boxing?"

My family said, "Yeah, we heard about it on TV."

I called Ed and sure enough, he said he'd decided to do something he'd always wanted to do. He said, "I have to find out now. If I don't find out now, I'll never know." I admired Ed for walking away from football where he was getting recognition. Relatively speaking, he was paid well. You had to respect him for giving that up to fulfill a dream. I respected Ed for making that decision and seeing it through, but I was also glad when he came back to football after boxing for one year.

We went to New York to play the Giants when he had his first fight. We tried to get to the hotel in time to see the fight on TV. Ed fought a guy named Yaki Manessis. Ed is 6'9" and Manessis was around 5'9". Ed rocked and rolled him in the ring and looked like a boxer. He didn't look like a football player anymore. He chased Manessis around the ring, tagging him and beating him. Ed slipped in the fifth round and in going down on one knee, he was eyeball to eyeball with Manessis. Manessis hit him hard while he was down. Ed was, like Sugar Ray says, "on queer street." He felt for the ropes and tried to get up. Luckily, the bell sounded, because Manessis was ready to get him. Ed went out for the last round and was still wobbly. He tried to grab Manessis, who was fighting like a kid in the street. Manessis wailed away trying to get in one more good shot. Ed made it through the final round and won the fight. He did, however, catch hell from his former teammates. We got him on the phone that night and started ragging him. We told him, "Boy, you'd better come back to football. You don't get hit that hard in football and at least you have a helmet on."

He said, "He caught me off guard. I was down and I didn't see it coming. He did sting me."

Ed had five more fights, then came back to football, and we were glad. Boxing turned out to be a blessing because when Ed came back, he was a better football player. First of all, he was in the best condition ever. Secondly, boxing had improved his hand speed and quickness. It also helped his longevity in the NFL. He was a well-conditioned athlete who took care of himself and did all the right things.

Ed was different off the field. He was the true bachelor. He had many lady friends that hung out with him. He and "Hollywood" Henderson opened a club called The Playmakers, on Knox and Henderson in 1977 after we won the Super Bowl. All we had to do was show up and girls would be waiting for us. Sometimes I spent the night at Too Tall's house and went to practice from there. He was single so it didn't matter to him, but I was married so it mattered to me. I told Coach Landry, "Tell my wife I stayed at the practice field all night." Of course, he wouldn't do that.

Ed is a close friend today. I have utmost respect for him; the way he did things and the way he carried himself, both as a player and in his life after football.

Thomas Henderson came into the league and evolved after two years with the Cowboys into **"Hollywood."** He was a character, that's for sure. He was a great athlete, one of the best I played with. He couldn't pick up a bat and hit a baseball; he didn't have the coordination to do that, or the coordination to shoot a basketball. If you gave him a basketball, however, he'd stand under the basket without a running start, and dunk the ball with two hands. If he ever hit a baseball, he was around the bases before you knew it.

He came from Langston University, which is not known for football players, let alone No. 1 draft picks. When he arrived in 1975, he and Randy White were both No. 1 draft picks. They were part of the Dirty Dozen class that made the team. Hollywood was by far the most flamboyant and outgoing, and the one who most enjoyed being a Dallas Cowboy. He didn't care where he was; he didn't mind talking about it. He liked being Hollywood. He loved signing autographs and played life to the hilt, loving every minute of it. We had to be careful that we didn't get caught up into his world, because we didn't need to be in it.

He was funny and told the best stories in the locker room. He was so graphic in his descriptions that you felt like you were there. He'd have the whole locker room mesmerized. The locker room was small, and we had one area that we called The Ghetto, where most black athletes dressed. The only white guy in it was Walt Garrison. He was in there whittling and dipping, so we had wood chips and snuff cans all over the place. Newhouse was a resident of The Ghetto, and the sloppiest teammate I ever played with. Most of his stuff was on the floor all of the time. Too Tall was a member of The Ghetto, and we had Mel Renfro, Benny Barnes, Calvin Hill, Tony Dorsett and Ron Springs at one time or another.

The Ghetto was where stories were told and where everyone hung out. We would lie on the floor, eat lunch and tell yarns. Thomas was the star of the party. He gave us graphic descriptions of what happened the previous night. God forbid, if you were with him, he would tell all of your moves to everyone. We rolled, cracked up, and had a good time. Those who weren't in The Ghetto, heard the stories. They snickered and laughed from around the corner.

The problem with Thomas was that he wanted to do everything his way. When he came to the Cowboys, they were the only team in the league using the flex defense. It was a defense based on discipline. You read your assignment and protected your area before you reacted to the ball. On other defenses, players were taught to react when the ball was snapped and make a play. But in the flex defense, when the ball snapped, you protected your area first, and then went to the ball. Thomas wasn't having any of that. He went to the ball no matter what. He was out of control and it frustrated people like Cliff Harris, Charlie Waters, and Lee Roy Jordan because they were perfectionists. D. D. Lewis and Dave Edwards couldn't understand Thomas. He had all that ability, so he got away with not yielding to the scheme of the defense.

Thomas was truly a rebel and ahead of his time. The more negatively the coaches talked about him, the more he did to get them to squawk. Instead of trying to correct it, he would rebel. Instead of succumbing and trying to get in line, he tried to get everyone in his line.

When the Cowboys finally let him go, Coach Landry had no choice. He found out Thomas was doing drugs. Some of his antics on the sidelines led Coach Landry to make an easy decision at a tough time. He cut Henderson before we were getting ready for the stretch run of the season. We had played the Redskins and Thomas did some crazy stuff on TV. Coach Landry heard about his antics after the game, then discovered that he was doing drugs in practice and during the games. This came as a shock to Coach Landry and to most players. Coach Landry cut Thomas in mid-stream. We had that stretch drive, about three games to play in December, before the playoffs. In letting Thomas go he sent a message to the team.

Coach Landry was no nonsense and felt that no one player was bigger than the team. He didn't put up with any crap. The players supported his decision to let Thomas go because we were playing a high-risk game in a high-risk business and we were there to win. Every time you stepped on that field, you expected your teammates to be ready. You didn't expect them to be on drugs. I dealt with Thomas later as a friend, but I was in the game to perform and to win. I wanted everything flowing in a positive direction with no one trying to bring us down and keep us from winning.

Thomas went to the 49ers, then to Miami where he broke a bone in his neck. Things spiraled out of control and led to jail time. But, if there is any teammate I'm most proud of in life after football, it's Thomas Henderson. He turned his life around. He has been sober for 21 years. Sometimes we have to hit rock bottom to see our way up. Thomas hit bottom. He was in jail, broke and friends had turned their backs on him. He came out of it, not because he hit the Texas lottery for $28 million and cashed out at ten million, but because of things he was doing before he won the lottery in 2000. He didn't become sober after he hit the lottery. He was sober years earlier. For him to go from where he was to where he is today, not having a drink or drugs in 21 years, is amazing.

Thomas is a fine person to be around now. He tells great stories but they're different kinds of stories. When you see him, you're proud of him. First, because he's alive, and the way he was going, he was headed for nothing but death. Second, he is at peace with himself and in control of himself and his life on a daily basis.

Preston Pearson came to the Cowboys in 1975 from Pittsburgh. We were looking for a running back. Prior to Preston, during my tenure with the Cowboys, they never made any trades. I called Preston "The Pro." He was the consummate teammate. His preparation was amazing. Preston wrote down every word out of Coach Landry's mouth in every meeting that he attended. This guy took notes while we were trying to stay awake or sneak something to eat. If there was any player I played with that I thought would become a coach in the NFL or college it was

Preston Pearson. It was because of the way he prepared for the game. He was always trying to absorb knowledge from Coach Landry and the rest of the coaching staff, and from the game itself. He was always serious; he never joked within the locker room environment. Preston had the locker next to me. He moved into Walt Garrison's old spot in The Ghetto. We did our ghetto talk, and Preston laughed, but he was more reserved than the rest of us. He was a serious person, a serious man about playing football.

Preston revolutionized the game. Coach Landry gave him a role and Preston turned it into a specialty — the running back as a receiver. It wasn't the normal shoot routes to sidelines. Preston took those simple routes and because of his ability, Coach Landry gave him the flexibility to run options. On some third downs, Preston had a defensive back covering him. He had the option of running it to the sideline or to break it inside. Roger would read Preston and hit him, usually for a first down. Preston would make the right decision because he was well prepared.

He was a third down specialist who came out of the backfield to make a play, and pick up a first down. In our offense, with Tony Hill and Drew Pearson on the outside and Billy Joe up the middle, we attracted most of the attention. That left Preston man to man on linebackers. After he started eating up linebackers, defense coordinators put safeties on him. After he ate up safeties, they put a cornerback on him. Now you had the nickel defense going with five defensive backs in the lineup. In some cases we faced six defensive backs.

I appreciated playing with Preston. Of course with the name Pearson, he couldn't be all bad. Though we're not related, we get that question all of the time. Everywhere he goes they call him Drew, and everywhere I go they call me Preston. His family is from Illinois and we're from the East Coast. When he met my family we talked about our heritage to see if there was a connection somewhere down the line. But there isn't any resemblance there. I'm a lot better looking.

You can't talk about **Cliff Harris** or **Charlie Waters** without talking about the other. They're that inseparable. They were different types of people. Charlie was more of an analytical type who wanted to know the whole picture before he did anything. With Cliff, it's "Let's just do it." Maybe that's why they got along so well together. If they were the same we wouldn't have needed both. They were coaches on the field. They knew their assignments and everyone else's. There were only three players I've played with that I thought had the ability to coach. They were Preston Pearson, Charlie Waters and Dennis Thurman. Charlie and Dennis coached and Dennis still coaches. Charlie coached at the college and pro level.

Cliff and Charlie were like bookends at safety. Cliff didn't have the greatest athletic ability but Charlie could hit a baseball, throw a football and shoot a basketball. Cliff couldn't do any of that as well. He was simply a football player. He would rather hit somebody than hit a ball. He had no finesse whatsoever as a basketball player. We played a lot of basketball in the off-season to stay in shape. We often played at Roger's house or at an aerobics center. When you played basketball with Cliff, you wanted him on your side, because sooner or later he was going to take you out.

They were extensions of Gene Stallings, the defensive secondary coach and Coach Landry. When you played the flex defense and constantly interchanged parts with new people coming in, you needed Cliff and Charlie to keep everyone in position and make sure they're in the right spot. They gave everything to the game mentally and physically.

It's amazing that they even had anything left in their lives after football.

Cliff played almost injury free but if he was hurt, he never complained. If he had any kind of injury, it was usually a head injury from sticking someone and ramming helmets together. He didn't wear wristbands and never pulled his socks up in a special way. He just put on his uniform and went out there and played football and did it to Hall of Fame caliber in my opinion. Cliff was inducted into the Ring of Honor at Texas Stadium and if anyone deserves this honor it's Harris.

Charlie wore a wristband or two and he was a different player than Cliff. He was a player who was always coming back from serious injuries. Both Cliff and Charlie were like me. They were overachievers.

Both came in the hard way. Cliff was a free agent. His success coming into the Cowboys as an undrafted free agent was a big reason that I signed with the Cowboys.

The hardest I was ever hit in practice was when Harris decked me on a Thursday before the Sunday game. Thursday was the day for defensive practice, so we were running scout team plays. I ran an in-route and Cliff laid me out flat. The trainers and everyone else came running. It was like somebody set off an alarm. I guess they thought I was dead because of the way he hit me. I don't think I moved. The trainers tended to me and we stopped practice. Coach Landry walked over and asked the trainer if I was all right. He said, "Yeah, I think he's alright. He'll be O.K."

Coach Landry said, "Just move the drill. We've got to get this practice in." This was the Thursday before the Sunday game. Cliff hadn't said anything. He didn't say he was sorry. He went to the next play.

Charlie sustained multiple injuries and had to overcome extended rehab to stay on the field. Sometimes before a game, I was in the locker room getting my ankles taped. When you came into the training room to get your ankles taped it was only a five — ten minute visit. When Charlie came in he'd be there for a while. He wouldn't go to the table to get his ankles taped; he'd go straight into the doctor's office. Three doctors, led by Dr. Pat Evans, were sitting there waiting for him. They had their needles lined up for Charlie. I had to leave because one time I watched him take a needle to his knee and his shoulder to play that particular game and it made me sick. To this day, he has back problems, an artificial knee, and problems with his hips, but, if you asked him if would do it again, he would say, "Yes."

Cliff and Charlie are friends in life after football. Charlie is an artist and does watercolor painting and pencil drawings. He drew a picture of the Hail Mary and sent it to me. In the note that he sent he wrote, "The day they saw ghosts." On the picture he put white faces on the Vikings fans in the stands. For him to do this for me shows the deep respect we have for each other.

I think we have mutual respect for each other because we know what we went through. We know the plays we made for one another. We know how Coach Landry worked us and drove us and made us cry; how he made us want to quit the game just to make us better. Because we went through it together, we have a special bond. Veterans of Iraq and Desert Storm have relationships that will last forever because of the time they spent together in the foxholes or in the camps. They know they can count on each other no matter what. We had that same relationship and bond as football players. You don't have that today with players moving around so much. When you play with guys eight to 10 years, you develop a bond and respect that carries through your entire life.

Mel Renfro, a Hall of Famer, was an outstanding football player and an even more outstanding person. Mel was part of The Ghetto but never said anything. He was quiet and just sort of laughed and went along with everyone. He was the type of person I looked up to. Even as a kid growing up, I liked Renfro, number 20. I liked the way he played the game. I always said when I watched him run: "Man, he could be a great wide receiver if they'd put him on the other side of the ball." His running style was natural, easy and fluid. I was so impressed with him that I used to steal his shoes from his locker. He wore the same size 10 as me and he had great shoes. I'd sneak into his locker – even before I made the team, when I went to the practice field to work out before training camp and I would steal his shoes. I put them back after I'd practiced. One pair I kept, and I think he knew they were his, but since I was working hard to make the team, he let me slide.

Mel was a blessing as a teammate because I was green as a wide receiver coming into the league. I needed all of the help I could get. Mel helped me. As a matter of fact, about a week or so before we left for camp, we were running routes on the practice field and he said to me, "Drew, I can tell what you're going to run every time you come off the line of scrimmage." I was devastated because it was a week before training camp and Renfro was telling me that he could read me like a book.

I asked him, "What am I doing wrong?"

He said, "You're leaning toward wherever you're going. Even when you run, you lean that way. When you're breaking to the right, you lean to the right. When you break to the left, you lean to the left."

I thought, *I better straighten that up, because I have the legendary Mel Renfro giving me a good piece of advice.* I worked hard and corrected the "leaning" before camp. I probably would not have made the team had it not been for Renfro. I'm glad he finally got into the Hall of Fame, even if it took too long for the committee to recognize his tremendous accomplishments.

Another great teammate was **Rayfield Wright**. Rayfield was part of the old school group, which included Bob Hayes, Jethro Pugh and Mel Renfro. I never heard Coach Landry or Jim Myers raise their voice at Rayfield. That was quite an accomplishment, because Myers raised his voice at everyone. He was Coach Landry's right arm and his disciplinarian as well. Anyone that could avoid Myers' wrath was doing a great job. Game in and game out, Rayfield did his job so effectively that he was never criticized. I have immense respect for the way he approached the game and played it. He was named to the Ring of Honor and there is no question that he should be in the NFL Hall of Fame. When you think of all of the things he did and the consistency with which he did it, he was the best offensive lineman who ever played for the Cowboys.

Tony Hill was my running mate. Tony came into the league as a rookie in 1977, the same year as Tony Dorsett. He was a third round draft choice. Dorsett came in with a Heisman Trophy and a national college football championship, yet he was quiet as he made his entrance into pro football. Tony Hill came in with hardly any credentials and talked more noise than anyone in Cowboy's history. He had tremendous confidence in his ability as a player. I guess he saw things out there on the first day of practice because he said, "Hey, I can be a starter on this team." He let everyone know he wanted to start. He talked a lot, but he backed it up with a tremendous career. I can still see Tony streaking down the sidelines and catching the long ball to help us win a game at the end. I remember a Washington Redskins game where we were down before half-time something like three touchdowns. It looked like a rout, and the next thing you know, in the second half, Tony caught three touchdowns from Danny White and we were back in the game. I liked to call him "instant offense" because he could make things happen quickly.

Tony always wanted the football. I used to call him Tony "Begging" Hill because he pleaded for the football. It wasn't easy to convince Coach Landry that you deserved the football. You couldn't go to him and say, "Hey, I'm open. Throw me the ball." Coach Landry wanted to know what defense, what down, what distance, what place on the field you were, and what hash mark before you told him you were open. Some people took it wrong, but I understood because Tony was just that way. He was aggressive in trying to make something happen. He wanted the ball and had that much confidence in his ability. He was a great compliment to me as a wide receiver. In fact he was the most effective running mate at wide receiver that I ever had. I started out with Bob Hayes, then there was Golden Richards, and then Tony Hill. As far as taking pressure and the concentration of the defense off me, no one did that better than Hill because he could get deep in such a hurry. I was the possession guy and Tony the game breaker.

Every Wednesday, before the next week's game, we came in for our Wednesday morning meeting and the first thing the coaches did was pass out the game plans. The first thing Tony and I did was go right to the passes and see who was going to be the featured receiver. You could tell by our reaction who *was* going to be the featured receiver because the one who wasn't was mad. However, we were never mad at each other. We both simply had tremendous confidence that we could make plays.

Even though my production went down when Tony came on

board, it was a blessing to play with him because he made us a better all-around team.

Golden Richards came in as "The Answer". He was supposed to be the heir apparent to Bob Hayes – the white hope; the white lightning. He was a good player, but hesitant because he had been hurt in college. While at the University of Hawaii, he tore up his knee against Grambling. Every time he caught the ball, it seemed as though he fell down instead of staying upright to take the licks. I think it was the effects of having gone through knee surgery. Golden worked hard. We were rookies together and my goal was to try to outshine Golden. He was the second round draft pick and got all of the attention. I knew the expectations that the Cowboys had for him. I thought that if I could out-perform Richards then I could make the team.

Golden was impressive for the first couple weeks of training camp. The thing that Golden had going for him was that he became good friends with Craig Morton right off the bat. Craig took a liking to Golden. This gave Golden the edge of having the quarterback on his side, calling him up most of the time to run a play when others were standing in line. Even though he had that going for him, there is no question that he made the team on his own ability. We played together three or four years before the Cowboys traded him to the Chicago Bears. That was a surprise to most of the fans in Dallas and me. When you were traded back then, it wasn't a good thing. It was usually for a negative reason. I think Golden had run his course in Dallas and when Tony Hill came in there was no question that Tony was a much better receiver than Richards.

Golden had some rough times in his life after football, but I've seen him recently at autograph sessions, and he looked great.

The heir apparent to Golden Richards, the second coming of White Lightning was **Doug Donley** from Ohio State. He was drafted in the third round. He had a bad shoulder, but he could run. I think he was faster than Richards, and in my estimation, a lot tougher. Because of the shoulder, Doug was limited. If you're a wide receiver, you need to be able to extend your arms above your head. Doug could not get one arm over his head. It was difficult for him to catch high passes. He was tough and the Cowboys liked him, so he made the team. I took him under my wing and we often hung out together. I tried to show him the ropes as a wide receiver. I tried to make him understand his role on the team, and what he needed to do to improve.

There is no question in my mind that Donley could have been a great wide receiver in the NFL if it hadn't been for his shoulder. It was puzzling that the Cowboys knew about the shoulder and drafted him as early as they did. That just showed what kind of ability the guy had. He was limited because he played behind Tony Hill, Butch Johnson and me. Here was a player with tremendous ability who never got a chance to showcase talent.

Butch Johnson was a character. When Butch came into the league I took to him and he took to me. We were good friends initially but, through competition, him wanting my job, and me not wanting to relinquish my job, that friendship waned. He began saying things about me in the newspaper. Of course I had to rebut to defend myself. Beyond that, I respected Butch because of the way he played the game.

He was the hardest hitting wide receiver I ever saw. Butch played wide receiver like a linebacker. He did not care who he blocked. We had blocking assignments on every running play. Sometimes we blocked the cornerback. That's when we got a break. Sometimes we blocked the safeties. Sometimes we blocked the linebacker on the end of the line and even the defensive end. I had a technique for each one of those positions. I whacked them if they weren't looking. But if they were looking, I didn't touch them. My philosophy was *live to play another day*. I preferred to hear Coach Landry yell at me than to be laid up in a hospital because some linebacker or defensive end decked me.

Butch didn't care if he blocked a cornerback, linebacker or defensive end. He blocked them all with the same intensity. He threw himself in there and annihilated whoever he was assigned to block He was a fearless wide receiver and I think Coach Landry liked his style because he kept trying to give Butch an opportunity to play.

Butch played behind me for eight years. He started messing with me and talking about taking my job. When he found out he couldn't do that, he started messing with Tony Hill and talking about taking Tony's job. Hill wasn't about to give his up, either. The coaches eventually designed a three wide receiver offense that turned out to be a tremendous asset to the overall offense. Now there was Drew Pearson and Tony Hill lined up on the outside demanding double coverage, and Butch Johnson around the middle with Billy Joe Dupree or Preston Pearson. Butch usually got man coverage and he ate that up. He ran tremendous routes and caught anything in the air that was near him because he had great hands.

Then he came up with the California Quake, and his dance in the end zone. It was O.K., but before Coach Landry put a stop to it, he was doing four acts of the California Quake after scoring a touchdown. It got to where Butch scored a touchdown, and Tony and I stood there with our arms folded just waiting for him to finish the California Quake so we could congratulate him.

He even went to clubs around Dallas with his California Quake.

He dressed in a tuxedo and did it on the dance floor. He should have left the California Quake on the football field because Butch wasn't a good dancer. But he was an effective receiver and a good teammate. Unfortunately, before it was over, we weren't good friends.

Before I had my accident in 1984, Butch demanded that the Cowboys trade him. He had done things that affected his relationship with Coach Landry and the Cowboy's organization. Even after my accident, they traded Butch to Houston. That's how bad the relationship had gotten between him the Cowboy organization and Coach Landry. I was gone and he could have easily stepped in as the starter. But the Cowboys traded him anyway. He burned his bridges before he left Dallas and ended up being traded to Houston. Houston cut him and Denver picked him up. He finished his career with the Denver Broncos.

He never was a starter in the NFL. His forte was as third receiver and that's what made Butch Johnson as an NFL player. He always thought that he should start, but it didn't happen for him.

Jethro Pugh was a quiet, good guy, and another pro who just came to play. All of the guys I came in early with: Lilly, Jordan, Lewis, Edwards, Neely, Nye, Niland, Fitzgerald and Manders approached the game as professionals. They never complained about the job, they went out and did it. They never complained about injuries. It was part of the game. When they were hurt, they dealt with it. Most of them played injured, including Jethro. Jethro always played hurt. Something was always hurt with Jethro whether it was a shoulder, leg or something else. He always played through it.

He and Rayfield and Bob Hayes were good friends. Bob, Jethro, Rayfield, and Cornell Green sat together on plane trips and played cards. They played from the time we took off until we landed. You could hear them arguing and making noise. Hayes was always the loudest. You knew when Bob was in the room, because he was the loudest.

Jethro was a great football player and another unsung hero for the Cowboys. He didn't get much recognition in his life after football, but the players that played with him and the coaches that coached him knew how great he was. Even the players that played against him knew how effective he was as a defensive tackle.

Bob Lilly was at the end of his career when I came in. I didn't know Bob in his prime, but he worked hard and was still Bob Lilly. When I was a rookie, he didn't show up for camp initially because he held out. The word was that he had found out over the summer that Alan Page of the Vikings made about $80,000. Bob's highest salary was about $50,000. Bob didn't have to play that year, because he'd had a great career and was Hall of Fame caliber. He wanted to extend his career but he was not going to do it for the same money. Lilly held out for the first couple of weeks of training camp and that was always the talk, the buzz. Players said, "When is Bob coming back? Is Lilly coming back?"

When he signed, we didn't see him around the team much. I guess part of his deal was to not live in the dorm. He lived somewhere off campus. We only saw him at practice and in meetings after he signed.

He was such a quiet gentleman all those years. The fact that he was underpaid hurt him. He never complained about it. I never heard Lilly complain about anything.

During his last year, he suffered a severe muscle tear on the inside of his groin. It was black and blue, an ugly tear. Yet he practiced every day. He taped up that leg and got treatment for it and still suited up every Sunday. Eventually the leg injuries caught up with him and he retired. I wish I could have played more seasons with Lilly because he wasn't only a great football player, he was also a great person. Lilly is the nicest guy I ever met. Fortunately, our paths cross often during our lives after football. He is forever friendly and cordial and always asks if there is anything he can do for me. That's Bob Lilly.

About the time that Jerry Jones took over the Cowboys, I was hosting a TV show, "Where Are They Now." The first person I interviewed was Lilly who was living in Graham, Texas. The camera crew and the producer were with me. Lilly was accommodating and the hospitality he showed us was extraordinary. He is a class person and it's no wonder they call him "Mr. Cowboy." Of all of the great Cowboy players I've played with, and the great guys on and off the field, nobody deserves the title of "Mr. Cowboy" other than Lilly. No other player would argue with you about that, either.

One of Bob's interests is photography. After we finished the "Where Are They Now" show and got ready to leave, Bob took one of his pictures off the wall, autographed it, and gave it to me. On the way back, we were supposed to talk about putting the show together, but all I could talk about was the picture. I held it in my lap all the way home and the picture of the Indian lady overlooking a canyon still hangs in my bedroom.

Lee Roy Jordan was like Lilly in many ways. He was the heart and soul of the team when I came. He was the spirit of the team, a vocal leader and leader by example. What surprised me was that he was too small to play middle linebacker in the NFL. The name, Lee Roy Jordan, is intimidating by itself. As an All America linebacker for Bear Bryant at Alabama, he approached the game with such intensity that it definitely heightened his presence as a player. If you weren't meeting that same intensity level, he let you know.

Jordan would grab you under the collar and straighten you out if you messed around. He was no nonsense. Roger was the leader on offense and Lee Roy took care of the defense. If you talked about an overall leader, there was no question that it was Jordan. He didn't take guff or fluff from anyone.

Rodrigo Barnes came in with me from Rice University and he was ahead of his time for sure. He thought that he should be the starting middle linebacker from day one in training camp. Here we were, running the flex and Jordan had been playing that system for double-digit years. Yet, Rodrigo thought he should start ahead of Jordan and he let people know that. He made the team as a rookie. There was one game where Lee Roy got hurt so Rodrigo started. He played a heck of a game. If he had left it at that, things would have naturally taken their course and he would have become the middle linebacker. But Rodrigo didn't have time for that. He told the coaches, the newspapers and everyone that he should be playing and that he was better than Jordan. Of course, there are certain things within the Cowboys that you don't mess with and Jordan was one of them. Eventually the Cowboys got rid of Rodrigo. He was one hell of a football player, but a little ahead of his time.

D. D. Lewis and **Dave Edwards** were pros, too. These guys played 10 or 11 years for the Cowboys before I got there. You looked at them in street clothes and thought there was no way they could play pro football. D. D. was short and slow. Edwards had the biggest calves I can remember, but he was also slow. But both were effective in the Cowboy's defensive scheme. They knew how to play the flex through long experience. The flex was designed for their abilities.

Edwards, whose nickname was Fuzzy, paced the sideline. His intensity level remained high whether it was practice or a game. He never sat still. When I think of Dave, I see him pacing the sideline, waiting to get back into the game.

They were the same kind of players. I don't think they would have been as effective on other NFL teams. They were products of the system, the style of offense and defense that we ran. They knew what they had to do and did it.

Robert Newhouse was a teammate I respected for the way he approached life and the game. Whether it was trying to improve himself as a football player or person, "House" was always doing something to better himself. Most of the time while he was with the Cowboys, he also went to college and worked to get his masters degree. Several of us went to school during the off-season but he also did it during the season. It was difficult to do that during the season but he did and never missed a beat. Robert's life after football has been very successful. He currently serves the Cowboys as director of player programs. Robert's son Rodd signed as a free agent with the Baltimore Ravens in 1998 and is currently with the Cardinals as the club's pro personnel assistant. His younger son Reggie, Baylor's career receiving leader, signed with the Cardinals as a free agent following the 2003 NFL Draft.

Tony Dorsett and I were inducted into the Texas Black Sports Hall of Fame the same year. During the induction ceremony I was the spokesman for the class and I remember saying that Tony had "a style of his own." As new backs come into the league the sports writers and fans always want to say that they run like Jim Brown, Eric Dickerson,

Walter Payton, or some other great running back. I've never heard them compare any new backs with Tony because Tony had "a style of his own." No one before or after ran with the same style as Tony.

Tony came in the league with high expectations from the fans. He had won the Heisman and played on a national championship team. During his career he exceeded all expectations and was named to the Hall of Fame.

For several years I had an annual banquet in New Jersey honoring my Dad and brother Carey. One of those years, I asked Tony to be the guest speaker. After he arrived, I found out that an uncle who was very close to him had passed away the day before. At a time that he understandably wanted to be with his family, he fulfilled his commitment to me. Even though I encouraged him to go on to Pennsylvania and be with his family, he stayed and made his speech. This is a prime example of the kind of person Tony Dorsett is.

When I think of **Randy White,** I think of every meeting we had after every game I played with Randy. Coach Landry would start each meeting with who played exceptionally well, then who played well and then who didn't play well. Without exception every meeting Randy White was in the category of "played exceptionally well." When we watched the game films they confirmed that Randy's performance was phenomenal every time he stepped on the field. Randy was big, tough, aggressive, committed and smart. He studied the game, knew his position, knew every position around him and executed with perfection. Because of his intelligence, this Hall of Famer, in his life after football, has been extremely successful.

Jay Saldi was one of my closest friends. We hung out together on and off the field and we knew each other's families. Jay was from White Plains, New York so we had the "East Coast thing" working. Jay came in as free agent and I didn't think he had a chance to make the team. I was just as wrong about Jay as a lot of people had been about me. He played in the NFL from 1976 to 1984 and played well. He played so well that Coach Landry devised an offensive formation for him (Jay Hawk). It was a formation that brought Jay in as a second or even third tight end. He was a hitter, devastating blocker, a playmaker and good friend.

Dick Nolan was the wide receiver coach the latter part of my career and one of my favorite people to be around. He was a laid-back kind of guy and at least gave the appearance of being easygoing. He had played for Coach Landry as defensive back with the Giants and, of course, was a head NFL coach for several years. I got close to him the year after I retired when I worked as his assistant wide-receiver coach. He not only taught me a lot about football, he also told tremendous stories that I could listen to all day long.   In 1991 Dick and I both became candidates for the head-coaching job with the Dallas Texans of the Arena Football League. Both Dick and I went through a series of interviews with the Texans and I couldn't believe it when I got the job over him.

As things turned out, through some arm-twisting on my part Dick agreed to be my assistant coach and mentor. He is truly one of my best friends and I enjoy and respect him as much as anyone I know.

Everson Walls, Ron Springs, Dextor Clinkscale, Michael Downs, Angelo King, Dennis Thurman and Ron Fellows all brought something special to the team. They were talented and worked hard.

Most of these guys were role players and were critical to our success. They were the young group, the new group and the now group. They considered the guys that came in prior to 1974 the old guys, brought a new aggressive element to the team, fit into the system and were all good football players.

Dan Reeves was the offensive coordinator. Of course, Coach Landry was the actual offensive and defensive coordinator. He was involved with every aspect of the game. But his right hand on offense was Reeves. What made Dan effective as a coach was that he had the same ability as Coach Landry to explain what he wanted you to do. Many coaches have innovative ideas, but they can't explain in a way that the players understand. Dan had that ability. I knew when Dan left the Cowboys that he would become a good NFL head coach because of his ability to make players understand what he taught.

During my last year with the Cowboys, 1983, I had a run-in with Reeves. It was during pre-season. This was my 11th year, so I knew how to work the pre-season. I knew the schedule. We usually played one quarter during the first game and gradually built up so that the veterans played three quarters in the final exhibition. This summer Butch was making noise and predicted on Channel 4 that he was going to take my job.

I came to camp ready. I was tight. I had ripples on my stomach and I didn't even drive to the practice field. I ran to the practice field and ran home after practice. I was ready to meet this challenge because Butch had come out publicly saying that he was going to win my job. I came into the camp in tremendous shape. I was ready and there was nothing Coach Landry could do to make me tired. I bulked up with weights and my upper body looked good. I never wore a shirt because I was proud of my physique.

We went through pre-season and everything was fine as far as the games were concerned. I followed the same pattern, and when we got to the last pre-season game, Reeves said, "Butch is going to start the second half."

I was pissed off, I said, "What?" I felt during training camp that Reeves was pushing Butch to be the starter. They had become buddy-buddy. You saw them talking all of the time. I was no dummy. I recognized these signs. I figured it had been Dan's call, not Coach Landry's, to start Butch in the second half. I didn't get in the game the second half and I fumed. When we got to the locker room after the game, I needed to talk to someone. I cornered Reeves and cussed and yelled at him. I said, "If you don't want me on this team, then get rid of me. I'm not going to be back up to anybody. I'm a star in this league and if you don't think I'm good enough to start with the Cowboys, then you need to let me go now."

I was ripping and yelling. All of the guys heard me, "What's with Drew?' they whispered.

This was a Saturday night game. The next morning I was lying by my pool reading the paper and chilling. The phone rang and Marsha said, "It's Coach Landry."

I said, "Oh God, I've been traded." I didn't want to take the call.

When I took the phone, Coach Landry said, "Drew, can you come see me?"

I asked, "When?

He said, "Now?"

I told Marsha, "Hey, I don't know what's going to happen, but Landry wants to see me." She knew I was mad and that I'd had a tantrum with Reeves. Apparently Dan had told Coach Landry about it.

I was in Coach Landry's office in a matter of minutes. In all of my years with the Cowboys, I'd never been in Coach Landry's office.

Their offices were located away from the practice field. Whenever we had to deal with Coach Landry or the other coaches, we dealt with them on the practice field. We never went to their offices.

I waited in the reception area. He even had his secretary working on Sunday. She told Coach that I was there but he made me wait a bit. When I got in and sat down, I had all of these things in the back of my mind that I was going to say to him.

The first thing he said was, "I understand you had a little run-in with Dan Reeves." Then he started explaining this and that. He talked about teamwork and being a good teammate. Before he finished his lecture, I was apologizing.

I said, "Coach, I'm sorry." I told him, "You'll never have any problem out of me again." I told him that I was embarrassed about him having to spend his time on a Sunday to deal with the situation. I said, "I'll never give you any more trouble ever again."

That's the way he was. If you went into a meeting with him furious, ready to pull no punches and to let him know what the deal was, you came out of the meeting apologizing. You wished you had never gone in there in the first place. I said, "I don't even know why I'm here. I'm a team player." I told him, "You're not going to have any problem out of me for the rest of the year. You don't have to worry about that." And he didn't.

I think my fuss with Reeves brought attention to what I was trying to do and the things I had done in the off-season to prepare myself for my eleventh year in the NFL. One thing about being slow is that you never lose speed. You stay the same. They couldn't say that I'd lost a step. Plus, I was always in tremendous shape, still making plays, and catching passes.

When I got home, Marsha was on pins and needles. We didn't

have cell phones back then, so I had to wait until I got home to tell her what had happened. I said, "I'm still on the team. Coach Landry and I worked it out." I told her, "I mostly just sat there and listened. Coach Landry told me what I needed to do to work it out."

Shortly after I had the run in with Dan, he became head coach at Denver and left Dallas. After Houston cut Butch, Denver picked him up.

I guess that getting upset with Dan had a positive impact because during the first five games, Coach Landry often called my name and number. I had around 30 catches. I was going across the middle, snagging passes with one hand. I was in great shape. I averaged six catches a game and wide receivers in the Cowboy offense normally didn't get that kind of production. Tony Hill and I figured that if we caught three to four passes a game for fifteen games; it was a solid season. To catch that many balls that early in the season was great. I was on my way to All-Pro. But shortly after that, the production, the opportunities and everything stopped. I think I ended the season with around 48 catches that year. So, I had 30 in the first five games and 18 the rest of the season. We were still winning though, so how could I complain?

I used to get in arguments with **Mike Ditka**. All Mike cared about was taking a guy's head off. He didn't care about pass routes or getting open. I'd say, "Mike, he's a linebacker."

He'd say, "I don't care. Just take his head off!"

I'd tell him, "Show me how to block him. Show me a technique."

His answer was, "Just run into him. Run into him and spread your feet and keep driving."

I never understood why they kept me in on short yardage and wanted me to be a key blocker. During a short yardage drill in practice one day, I lined up off the tight end and Billy Joe was supposed to set up the defensive end. My job was to stymie him and hold that position so we could go outside. The defensive end was Too Tall. Billy Joe stood him up and slid off on the linebacker. I came in, and Too Tall knocked the crap out of me. He threw me away like I wasn't there and the play got stopped for no gain. This was a drill in practice on Friday before a Sunday game. Ditka laid into me. I yelled back at him, "Why the heck do you want me to block that defensive end? If you want me to block him, teach me a technique. Show me how to do it." We went at it face to face. Consequently, they took me off that team. I didn't have to block anybody because I wasn't there any more on short yardage. They got the picture and put the third tight end in on that wing and let him block the defensive end. Then the play started to work.

Mike and I stayed at odds with each other. We argued all the time. No one got up for a game more than Ditka. The only problem with that was that he wasn't playing. He chewed gum like he was tearing it up and paced the sideline pulling up his pants. He had only recently retired as a tight end, so he knew many defensive players. He yelled at them during the pre-game warm-up. Kenny Reeves from St. Louis was a nemesis when Mike played. He ragged Kenny, called him "sorry", and told him, "We're running right at you." Mike was pretty fired up.

The other coaches said, "Mike, shut up. You'll get these guys pissed off."

I tried to block on one play and Kenny Reeves decked me. Then he said, "You go take that to Ditka."

I told Ditka, "Mike, you're killing me."

He also ragged on Bill Bradley of the Eagles and Kenny Houston with the Redskins all of the time. These were physical guys. You didn't want to start something with those guys. It was tough enough playing against them without your coach on the sideline talking noise.

I remember that I got knocked out in a Pittsburgh game in the first quarter. Dennis Winston from Arkansas, who was nicknamed "Dirt," played middle line backer instead of Jack Lambert. When we arrived in town the newspapers said "Lambert out for Cowboy game." We thought, "Alright, maybe we'll finally beat these guys." We were excited that we would be able to run on them. I ran a slant pattern that receivers call the suicide route — five yards up field and break into the teeth of the defense. What you hoped was that the quarterback hit that hole. If he didn't hit that first hole, and God forbid missed that second hole, you would get hit. Roger missed me on the first hole, and threw it to me in the second hole. Winston decked me. I went flying, hit my head on that hard turf in Three Rivers Stadium, and was knocked out. I was coherent as far as being able to get up, but I didn't know where I was.

When I got to the bench, all I heard was yelling. Ditka yelled at me but I couldn't hear what he said. I saw him, but he was a blur. He kept saying, "Get back in there. Don't take a lick like that." I was half dead, but that's how intense he was. For the rest of that game he was jawing at all of the Steelers, Winston, Donnie Shell, Mike Wagner and Mel Blount. He irritated them. I went back into the game, we ran that same play in the fourth quarter, and the same thing happened. Winston knocked me out again. The ironic thing was that Roger also got knocked out. He was scrambling and I came back to block but I couldn't get there in time to stop L.C. Greenwood. He put his helmet in Roger's chest and drove him to the turf. That was a hard hit in itself, but what knocked Roger out was when his head hit the turf. You could see it bounce. Roger was out until we were on the plane heading back to Dallas. When he came to and asked what happened, I said, "Game's over. We're heading back. We got beat by Pittsburgh again."

LANDRY

CHAPTER THIRTY
★★★★★

I've talked a lot about Coach Landry in this book. I am going to sum up my remarks about him by taking the liberty to quote myself with the words I said at his memorial service on February 17, 2000 at the Meyerson Symphony Center in Dallas.

"When I got word of Coach Landry's death and passing…I felt that, deep within my heart, I needed my own time in my own place, by myself, to grieve over the loss of someone that I loved, someone that I admired and someone that I respected so much.

"Through the course of my grieving, my thoughts ran through the gamut of emotions. I felt shock, I felt denial, I felt anger, I felt confusion, I felt frustration, I felt fear, I felt helplessness, I felt numbness. But eventually, through all that, I felt a sense of acceptance.

"I was at a point of not knowing what to do but wanting to do something. Then I realized that there really is no death. There really is no end. There is only transformation. Coach Landry has now made that transformation. He now exists in a new time, in a new place, in a new reality, and because of that, so do we.

"The relationship I had with Coach Landry has now transformed from the physical to the spiritual. But it certainly hasn't ended; it has only changed. And instead of talking to him face-to-face, eyeball-to-eyeball, I now communicate with him through prayers. And by grieving, I was able to release the negative thoughts and negative emotions that make it easier to accept this change.

"I also found out that grief is natural, it's normal, and it's to be expected. I further realized that I owed it to Coach Landry to grieve and to cleanse my soul of those negative thoughts…so I could accept this transformation…

"I can't believe I played the game, pro football, in a league, the NFL, for a team, the Dallas Cowboys, for a coach, named Tom Landry. And I don't need any honors like the Ring of Honor or the Hall of Fame to accentuate or punctuate my career. What accents and punctuates my career more than anything is the fact I played 11 years for Coach Tom Landry. You can't get any more respect than that.

"When my children, and recently my grandchildren, ask me about my playing days in the NFL, I won't tell them about my catches or touchdowns, or even the Hail Mary. I'll simply say: 'I played 11 years for Coach Tom Landry.' And because they will know about Coach Landry and about his great success as a coach and about his great success as a person and they will also know about the great legacy that he has left, I suspect my children and grandchildren's response will be: 'Man, you must've been a good player to play for such a man for 11 years.'

"If I know Coach Landry like I think I do, he's probably up there in heaven right now trying to start his own football league. He'll probably call it the GFL----God's Football League. Of course, the team will be called the Dallas Cowboys, and we all know why that hole in the roof is there at Texas Stadium: so God can watch his team.

"He'll probably select Clint Murchison as his owner. He'll probably select Vince Lombardi as his offensive coordinator, George 'Papa Bear' Halas will probably be his defensive coordinator, and we must all believe that one or two Washington Redskins have made it to heaven, so he'll probably pick George Allen as his special teams coach.

"And you can bet that he's already recruited Mark Tuinei, Walter Payton and Derrick Thomas as players. And because he's looking for new recruits all the time, we all better beware and we all better get qualified to play in this new league.

"To qualify for the GFL, you don't have to be big, you don't have to be strong and you don't have to be fast. But what you do have to do is live your life according to God's standards. And you had better put all your faith and trust into the Lord, because if you don't, you'll never get the opportunity to play for Coach Landry and the GFL.

"One final thing. You know, in life, sometimes we don't get the opportunity to tell a loved one how we really feel about them. And I really feel blessed that I had the opportunity to tell Coach Landry before he passed on how I felt about him. Face-to-face, eyeball-to-eyeball, I told him simply what he meant to my life, how he's changed my life----through all the good times, through all the bad times----how he always seemed to have been there for Drew Pearson. I feel blessed that I had the opportunity to tell him those things.

"We're all going to miss Tom Landry, but we all know that if we do the right thing and live our lives the way he did, we'll have that opportunity to meet him again."

EPILOGUE

EPILOGUE
★★★★★

It has been nearly 30 years since I caught the Hail Mary pass and 21 years since I played my last football game. My ability to catch a football opened many doors for me and I thank God everyday for that gift. I have been afforded the opportunity to live out what most people only dream of.

My life today has changed. I don't run the frantic pace that I once did. I run only when I have to. There was a time when I didn't take time for my family or myself. I didn't take time to enjoy doing the things I wanted to do and the things we needed to do as a family.

I said yes to everyone. I didn't want to let anyone down, so most of my time was spent fulfilling other people's needs or requests. I remember Coach Landry saying to the team back when I was a rookie. "One of the hardest things to learn in this business is how to say no." As usual he was right. The only time I was home was when my schedule allowed it.

Now I am more selective in what I do and I've learned how to say no. I find alternative ways to continue to help people and fulfill their requests. I have found ways to do this without a physical presence. I stay home so I can spend time with my son Jared and grandsons Duce and Toren. Despite missing valuable time with my two daughters while they were growing up, we are blessed to have the opportunity to make up for it now.

When I examine my accomplishments in life, I am most proud of endeavors related to my children. I am proud of putting my two daughters, Tori and Britni, through college and proud because they always make good decisions and do the right things. My son, Jared, is one really cool kid. He plays the violin and is a member of the Greater Dallas Youth Orchestra. His interests are a little different than mine and he has taught me to appreciate some things other than sports.

The Pearson family has suffered many tragedies in the past four years. Heart attacks took my brother Sam in October 2000 and our mother in February 2001. Two weeks after Mom died my Aunt Ethel passed away. Six months later, at the age of 44, my baby sister Debbie passed away from cancer. While all this was happening to the family, I lost my best friend, Harvey Martin on Dec. 24, 2000, and Bob Hayes in 2001. My sister Denise also was diagnosed with breast cancer and the only reason she is a survivor today is because of early detection. She got a check up after Debbie was diagnosed. Most recently, my brother Andre is battling prostate cancer.

As a result of the events around me, I was disheartened but did not know I was suffering from depression. I thought I was just down and out from all that had happened. I noticed difficulty controlling my feelings and emotions. I didn't want to be around people. I could feel myself going into a complete shell. I became frustrated from not being able to do anything about it.

An article in *Sports Illustrated* on depression and professional athletes saved me. As I read the article and realized how depression affected the lives of Terry Bradshaw and Ricky Williams, I thought, *This sounds like me.*

After reading the article I realized that I needed professional advice. I contacted Dr. J.R. Zamorano. He was the Dallas Cowboys team physician when I played and is still involved with the Cowboys.

Dr. Zamorano said he could see the sadness in my eyes and it was apparent that I was suffering. We talked and I told him about the personal tragedies. We discussed the symptoms of depression and he told me my problems were deep rooted, resulting from my car accident and the death of my brother Carey.

Since then I've been combating this disease through medication and personal spiritual growth and there is no question that I am better. Through tragedy and triumph I have received several Hail Marys. I consider learning to overcome recent hardships and the opportunity to tell my story as two of them.

Most everyone's life is challenged by difficult odds but I believe that everyone gets a few Hail Mary's and that if we work hard and prepare ourselves, we might catch a few of them.

Hail Mary
★★★★★

MEMORIES

Most Athletic
South River High

Scotty Skarzynski
my favorite receiver

Baseball
my favorite sport

Tulsa Quaterback 1970

Marsha and I married in Tulsa

Cardinals 1974
Best Catch I ever made

Touchdown
Jets 1975

Dad

Drew and Mom

Moose

Sam, Andre, Mom, Drew, Sandra, Denise, Debbie, Kyle

My favorite picture
Britni, Tori

My Girls
Tori and Britni

My Grandboys
Duce and Toren

My Boy
Jared

Four Generations of Athletes
Drew, Kavika, Duce, Marques

Best Friend
Harvey

Super Bowl
New Orleans - 1977
Family and Friends

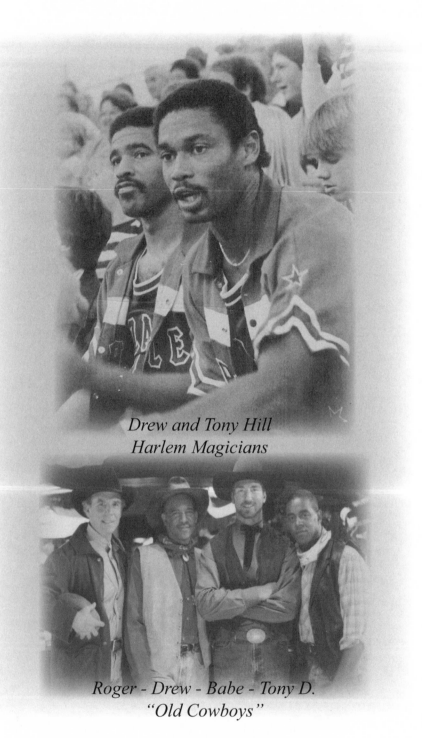

Drew and Tony Hill
Harlem Magicians

Roger - Drew - Babe - Tony D.
"Old Cowboys"